Teacher Absent Often

Building Sustainable Schools from the Inside Out

Kari Grady Grossman

Adapted for youth by
Jennifer O'Neal Michel
from the original,
Bones That Float, A Story of Adopting Cambodia

Wild Heaven Press

Teacher Absent Often: Building Sustainable Schools from the Inside Out
Copyright © 2012 Kari Grady Grossman.

All Rights Reserved. No part of this book may be reproduced, stored in a retrieval system or transmitted in any form or by any means, electronic, mechanical, scanning, photocopying, recording, or otherwise without prior written permission of the copyright holder, except brief quotation used in a review. For more information, please contact Wild Heaven Press, PO Box 707, Fort Collins, Colorado, 80522.

First Edition

Map design by Anne Austin

All images courtesy of © George and Kari Grady Grossman

Grady Grossman, Kari
 Teacher Absent Often: Building Sustainable Schools from the Inside Out / Kari Grady Grossman.
 —1st ed.

ISBN-13: 978-1-4701776-4-5
ISBN-10: 1-4701776-4-1

Library of Congress Control Number: 2012904133

Wild Heaven Press, PO Box 707, Fort Collins, Colorado 80522 USA
wildheaven.com

Printed in the United States of America

Dedicated to

Paul Chuk
for turning my vision into reality,

and Sem Kong
our first college graduate.

Acknowledgements

This book is the brainchild of some very special educators who, after reading my first book *Bones That Float,* came to me and said, "we want to teach this book in our middle school classrooms." I'm thrilled, that with this youth edition, Cambodia's story will at last be taught in schools.

My heartfelt thanks to Nikki Stansfield, curriculum coordinator at Lincoln IB World School, and Monique Flickinger, technology coordinator at Poudre School District, for their belief in this project and for offering their educator's eye to the manuscript. Thank you to Jennifer O'Neal Michel for helping translate my thoughts into words and tenses that middle school students can relate to. I am grateful to the Bohemian Foundation of Fort Collins for their financial support to create both the youth book and the accompanying Make Change Matter service-learning program.

My good friends Michele and Mike Wetzberger provided a wonderful cabin in the mountains where I could work undisturbed by the demands of raising two young children and running an international development organization. That organization, Sustainable Schools International, would not be alive today without the dedication and expertise of its outstanding board members who took a leap of faith with this project: Mona Thornton, Ellen Gordman, Jeanne Sirkin, and Andy Fenselau.

I appreciate the volunteer input of Launie Parry, our graphic designer, Jason Kuri our website programmer, and Joni Martin an outstanding third grade teacher who allowed her students to be our test pilots.

I am deeply humbled by the hard work and perseverance of my colleagues Paul Chuk, Sem Kong, Nigm Sobun, Tau Soka, and the teachers and villagers of Chrauk Tiek who believed.

And lastly, behind it all is George, my husband, my counsel, my strength, without him nothing happens.

Contents

Map of Cambodia x
Prologue: A River Like Me xiii

Part one
Adopting Cambodia

1 Family 3
2 Ratanak's Short History 7
3 Exploring Cambodia 9
4 A New Friend. 13
5 Adoption Decree. 17

Part two
A Child of the Khmer Rouge

6 The Irish Jewish Cambodian Cowboy. 21
7 A Cambodian Wedding in Wyoming. 23
8 Amanda's Kitchen. 29
9 Amanda's Childhood 33
10 The Long March. 37
11 The Year Zero 39
12 Remembering Little Sister 41
13 Half-Moon Cake 49
14 Daikon Camp 53
15 Escape 57
16 Refugee 61

Part three
Teacher Absent Often

17	Building A School	67
18	Teacher Absent Often	71
19	The Letters	79
20	Lessons Learned	89
21	Human Resources	97
22	A Change of Attitude	105
23	Dreams Grow Bigger	113
24	Five Core Values	119
25	Wash Hands Soap	125
26	Expansion	131
27	Seeds of Change	137
28	The Return	143
29	The Secret to Sustainability	151

Epilogue	155
Make Change Matter	156
Author Bio	158
Bones That Float	160

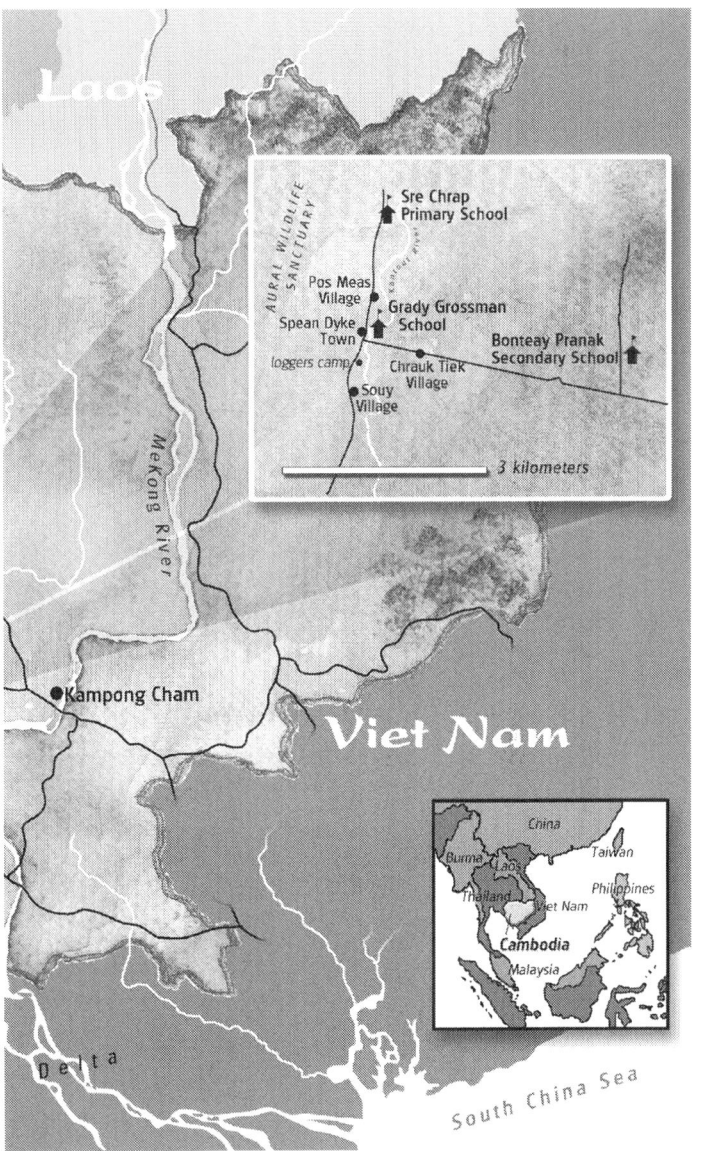

Prologue

A River Like Me

The river is flowing backward, my first clue that Cambodia is going to show me a new perspective. In the middle of the rainy season, the Tonle Sap River helps the swollen Mekong River drain slowly into the ocean by absorbing the overflow and reversing its course. This river is like me: taking in Cambodia from two different directions, two different outlooks—as an American mother and as an adopted mother of Cambodia.

On the far side of the river, a fisherman casts his butterfly net into the water while his son poles their boat, called a sampan, under the bronze glow of thick, sun-drenched clouds. At the water's edge, two small children fight like beasts over a loaf of French bread. Near me, a man with an amputated leg holds out a blackened baseball cap for my donation; his tattered shirt has a McDonald's logo on the pocket. I feel a knot in my stomach.

The knot has been there since my heart found its way to Cambodia in March 2001, when my husband, George, and I adopted our son, Grady, at an orphanage outside the capital city of Phnom Penh. My river was flowing downstream then, toward family and future. Yet the current changed its course that day, when an eight-month-old boy crawled into our arms and Cambodia's story crawled in with him. Our lives were unexpectedly rocked by the ripple effect of a war, many years past, that defined my new son's life and circumstance. Today Cambodia is a country of fourteen million people, half of them under the age of eighteen. One out of every eight Cambodian children either will die before the age of five or be orphaned before turning fifteen.

Two lives twist and untwist with mine in this book. One of them escaped from Cambodia and realized her dreams in America; the other didn't. Amanda Prom, my friend, was once a little girl called Maly. She survived the horrors of the war in Cambodia and rebuilt her life in small-town Wyoming, where she runs a Chinese restaurant. Sovann Ty, a taxi driver who helped me build an education project, never escaped Cambodia. He continues to navigate through violence, poverty, and corruption toward an uncertain future. He hopes that one day he, too, will touch American soil.

When my husband and I adopted a little boy, and in turn adopted his country, we discovered a connection in our souls to a little known and long-suffering people. This book is about the journey we made in adopting and raising our son and how, through his story, we became inseparably connected to his birth country, Cambodia.

part one

Adopting Cambodia

"Adoption carries the added dimension of connection not only to your own tribe but beyond, widening the scope of what constitutes love, ties, and family. It is a larger embrace."

Isabella Rossellini, adoptive parent

chapter one

Family

Kari and her husband, George, were a strong, healthy young couple. Together they had ridden bicycles three thousand miles to Alaska, climbed mountains, paddled rivers, and started a business. After several years together, they felt it was time to start their family. They wanted to begin the next stage of their life and have a baby. But it didn't happen.

Kari felt stuck and frustrated. She felt like the next stage of life was waiting for her, but the door to it was locked. So they started to research their options. After a lot of time, money, and medical procedures trying to overcome infertility, George and Kari decided it was time to let go of the desire to have biological children and open their hearts and minds to the world of possibility. They chose international adoption.

Adopting a child is a long, complicated, and stressful process, as Kari and George soon discovered. They filled out forms, waited, filled out more forms, and waited some more. From the beginning, they knew that the child's country of origin and race really didn't matter; they didn't care if their child looked like them—they just wanted to be a family. To ease her stress and anxiety, Kari began meditating every day, asking the energy of her heart to radiate toward their child, wherever he or she was. Why wait for a child to be born in America and to be selected by a birth mother, they reasoned, when they could give their love to a child in an orphanage who was already waiting for a family?

George and Kari knew several couples who had adopted Chinese girls, so they joined their communication network. One day, one of the families in the network sent them an email about children waiting for parents in Cambodia. When Kari read that simple message, she felt like a gentle, invisible hand took hold of her heart. At that moment Cambodia, a country she had never seen, infused its traditions and its troubles into her life forever. She began researching Cambodia, learning about its history and culture, and the adoption process. After two weeks making phone calls and searching the Internet on the computer, Kari felt so overwhelmed by all the information that she called her mother for advice.

"Mom, I just learned about orphaned children in Cambodia," she said.

From her kitchen in Maine, Kari's mother replied, "Cambodia—you're kidding me! I just got back from the beauty parlor, where I met a woman who told me all about the adoption process in Cambodia."

Kari's mother had written down the names and phone numbers of the exact same people Kari had already been calling and emailing during her two-week fact-finding mission. During the conversation, George came into the room with the mail and showed Kari the new issue of *National Geographic*. The cover story was about Cambodia. Kari knew they were headed in the right direction.

On December 18, 2000, Kari and George received word of a five-month old boy who had been living at an orphanage near Phnom Penh, the Cambodian capital, for several months. His name was Ratanak and they knew instantly that this child was their son. Three days later, they received a picture and a one-page fax that told them his height and weight and described his health as "good."

With little debate, they faxed back their acceptance of the child, but they had no idea when they would be able to see and hold Ratanak and make him theirs officially. Kari and George waited three months while the slow wheels of the adoption process turned in Cambodia. Their faith was strained while they waited, but Kari nurtured her boy from afar, watching over him in her mind and heart. She kept telling herself it would all happen in time.

When the phone call finally came, George and Kari were on a plane and headed to Cambodia only three days later. When they arrived at the Roteang Orphanage outside of Phnom Penh and met Ratanak for the first time, it wasn't love at first sight. How could it be? They were in a room with fifty gorgeous children, all younger than two.

The details of how each child came to be in the orphanage were unique, yet the causes were similar: some parents had died; some babies were foundlings; others were given up by family members simply because they didn't have enough food to feed them. Kari and George were grateful that someone else chose Ratanak for them, because they would never have been able to choose among so many beautiful children, all in need of a family to love and raise them.

George and Kari quietly watched Ratanak as he interacted with the nannies and other children. He was quiet and introverted. He was eight months old—clean, toothless, and chubby. He didn't babble, he didn't eat solid foods, and he didn't crawl. Kari secretly wondered if there might be something wrong with him.

Then the orphanage nannies asked George and Kari if they liked the baby. They were eager to please and appeared ready to exchange him for another child. Kari felt a sudden protective urge in her gut and said, "Yes, we like him! Absolutely!"

A Cambodian Buddhist monk offers a traditional family blessing over Kari, George and their new son, Ratanak.

chapter two

Ratanak's Short History

One thing definitely sets adoptive parents apart from those with a biological child: adoptive parents face the possibility that their child will want to search for his or her birth family one day to answer basic questions such as "who do I look like?" and "where does my talent come from?" Kari felt that raising Ratanak wasn't just about giving him love and a stable home environment, but it was also about giving him the truth of his heritage if and when he asked for it.

Kari and George learned some details about how Ratanak had come to be in the orphanage from a nanny who remembered the day of his arrival. She said that a woman came to the door of the orphanage, alone, with three children in tow—a baby boy, a little girl, and a ten-year old boy. This mother was taking her oldest boy to the free hospital in Phnom Penh and needed the orphanage to take care of her baby while she was gone. Two days later, she returned with only the little girl; the older boy had died. She begged the orphanage to keep the baby because she had no food for him. Her husband was also dead.

The barely literate nanny had scratched the details onto a piece of paper the size of a napkin. At the bottom of this short description, the woman and the nanny had put their thumbprints to witness the document. This was all George and Kari knew about Ratanak's history.

Nannies taking care of the babies at Roteang Orphanage. Ratanak is on the left.

chapter three

Exploring Cambodia

Kari knew it would take time for the baby to bond with her and George, so they visited the orphanage every day to spend time with Ratanak. They didn't want to remove him from the orphanage until all the paperwork was complete and finalized, so he stayed in the care of his nanny for five more weeks.

Between visits to the orphanage, George and Kari decided to explore the countryside and take pictures to make a scrapbook for Ratanak, so they could show him his birth country of Cambodia as he grew up in America. However, they weren't sure which images of Cambodia they wanted to capture. The ancient stone temples? The luscious, tropical beauty? Or the miserable conditions that lead to thousands of orphaned and abandoned children? They found the answer to their question in a place they never expected—in the person of a charming moto taxi driver named Sovann Ty.

Motos, a common form of transportation in Cambodia, are miniature motorcycles with long seats that are cheap to operate and easy to maneuver through crowded streets. Moto taxi drivers are a dime a dozen in the city of Phnom Penh, lingering on every street corner and badgering passersby to take a ride. The moto drivers desperately wanted to earn US dollars, and George and Kari became accustomed to their endless offers of rides, goods, and favors, but mostly ignored them.

But one day, as they were standing outside the Royal Palace of King Sihanouk, pondering a map of the city, Sovann approached them. He was different. With two easily understood English phrases—"Where are you going? Can I help you?"—he got their attention. They dropped their guard and began asking Sovann a countless number of questions. His friendly conversation and genuine assistance were a welcome alternative to the other moto drivers and for about seventy-five cents he offered to take them anywhere they wanted to go in the city. As a bonus, he also offered to act as their interpreter and their guide.

Every day after that, George and Kari squished themselves Cambodian-style onto the long banana seat of Sovann's red moto. As he eased into the never-ending flow of vehicles, they became a part of the lifeblood of the city. Cars with steering wheels on either the right or left side merged with trucks of all sizes, motos, bicycles, pushcarts, and any other kind of wheeled vehicle that could possibly transport people, pigs, produce, bamboo, chickens, or all sorts of other things. They all fought for a place in the transit hierarchy. The occasional stop sign or traffic light was largely ignored; a honk and a flash of the headlights communicated the ever-changing rules of the road. The governing principle seemed to take its cue from the social structure of Cambodia itself: he who is bigger wins.

Even though most of the vehicles were open, hardly anyone wore a helmet. Whole families squeezed onto a single moto: one child between the handlebars and another on the gas tank, the father driving with a toddler between his knees, the mother riding sidesaddle with a baby on her hip. Once Kari counted eight people on one moto! The adoption agency had warned Kari and George *not* to ride motos; to be safe they should hire a car and driver. But they liked the energy they felt being in the streets with everyone else. They felt more connected to humanity and to real life in Cambodia.

Kari reassured herself that her child already had lost one set of parents—surely he wouldn't be subject to the same fate twice. "Are there a lot of accidents?" she asked Sovann.

"My mother died instantaneously in the street!" he shouted over his shoulder to her. Then he explained that his mother had been riding sidesaddle on a moto taxi, returning from her sister's funeral, when a truck hit them. At the scene, the driver of the truck paid off the policeman with a few thousand riels (Cambodian dollars). Sovann couldn't afford to buy a meeting with a judge to bring the truck driver to justice, so he just let the matter drop.

"No good law," he said. "Cambodia very corrupt."

Over the course of their five-week wait to adopt Ratanak formally, Kari and George spent many hours riding on Sovann's moto taxi around Phnom Penh. They sped past a mixture of ancient, colonial, and modern architecture. Everything needed a paint job. The grime-covered walls, chipped by bullet holes, hid a glorious and cruel history. The time when the international press referred to Cambodia as "the jewel of Asia" was long gone.

Thousands of shanties were crammed between dirt alleyways; naked street children and limbless beggars signified how far the country had fallen. Kari and George were both joyful to discover something beautiful in the city but also saddened by its dereliction and neglect.

The weeks George and Kari spent riding on the back of Sovann's moto taxi gave them an experience of Cambodia that none of the travel books prepared them for. Although Sovann's tendency to move around the city as he wished strained their patience, they remained loyal customers because the relationship was mutually beneficial. They appreciated his independent mind when most other locals seemed passive around tourists. Sovann recognized that adoptive parents were a new kind of client and he wanted to make them happy. He had a talent for showing them the real people and culture of Cambodia in an honest, open way.

chapter four

A New Friend

The night Kari and George met Sovann, he had asked, "Do you want to eat real Khmer food?" On the back of his moto, they crossed the Tonle Sap River and found themselves at the Heng Neak restaurant, where Khmer food was served in traditional style. It was a restaurant unlike any Kari and George had ever seen before. A large, tin roof staked a claim to a patch of jungle beside the river. Under it, a tile floor hosted a hundred long tables neatly set for dinner but mostly empty. A high-pitched karaoke singer was belting out a tune on the stage at one end. The sun had set, and the temperature had dropped from a sweltering one hundred degrees to a relatively cool ninety. As they sat at their table, a refreshing breeze wafted over a bamboo partition separating the seating areas from the jungle.

A swarm of colorful teenage girls greeted George and Kari at their table, each wearing a sash from shoulder to hip. A small boy in dirty shorts pointed to Kari's shoes, while a dutiful young girl held out a plate of white jasmine flowers. Their faces were insistent, so George bought Kari the flower necklace, and she let the little boy give her old, worn-out sandals their first polish. When George tried to tip the girl who had kept their glasses full of beverages the entire evening, Sovann said, "No pay her. The company pay her to sell their product."

"How much do they pay?" asked George.

"Maybe one dollar per day."

"Is that enough to live on?"

"Not really."

Steaming piles of rice arrived, alongside vegetables and soup that smelled at once sour and hot, salty and sweet. The smells overwhelmed their taste buds. Kari found that the loud karaoke music gave her a headache, and she started to lose her appetite. Instead of eating, she focused her attention on Sovann as he devoured his meal. The churn of his facial muscles crunching food between his high cheekbones and sharp, square jawline mesmerized her. He was a very thin man, and Kari imagined him being able to slip through the cracks in the bamboo slats.

Finally, she had to ask, "Where do you put it all?"

Sovann looked up with a sheepish grin and mumbled, "It's in my cheeks." And it certainly was! The pouches of both cheeks were filled to capacity with rice. He wiped the corner of his mouth and swallowed. "During communist regime, not enough food. Save, eat later." He quickly started eating again as though he didn't know where his next meal would come from.

As George and Kari got onto Sovann's moto for the ride back to the hotel, a storm came in. Great sheets of heat lightning rumbled across the sky, and electric-blue streaks outlined the storm clouds. With each flash, the clouds appeared as explosions of light against the dark sky. The night was alive, and they were immediately soaked in the pouring rain as Sovann made his way across the Japanese Friendship Bridge and back into the city. Through the dense rain, it was hard to see the headlights and taillights of the other vehicles around them—if they had lights at all. The tension of several close calls was softened by the wetness, a refreshing break from the dismal heat of the day. For the first time, Phnom Penh struck Kari as beautiful.

From that night on, Sovann would become Kari's agent in Cambodia. For the next eleven years, Kari would work with him to help children left behind in this beautiful, impoverished country inflicted by a painful past that was still very much a part of the present.

Sovann (with baseball hat) buying supplies from a Phnom Penh vendor.

chapter five

Adoption Decree

Five weeks after George and Kari arrived in Cambodia, they were issued an adoption decree for their son; finally it was time for Ratanak to leave the orphanage. At the embassy, they had to take an oath that they would have the baby vaccinated. Weighing the pros and cons was not an option. What difference did it make anyway? They knew their child had already run the gauntlet of deadly diseases during the most vulnerable days of his life—tuberculosis, polio, typhoid, malaria, hepatitis, parasites, and AIDS—all of them rampant in Cambodia. Kari knew her new son was strong.

Within two days, Ratanak was crawling across the floor of their hotel room, pulling himself up on things, babbling for attention, and laughing when he got it. Like most first-time parents, Kari and George felt unsure of themselves, but they were also in a foreign country and far away from anyone who could instruct them on baby care and maintenance. They had to trust their instincts and discovered quickly that loving children doesn't come from how much they look like you; it comes from figuring out how to take care of them.

At last they had Ratanak's immigration visa and boarded a plane at Pochentong International Airport, bound for their Wyoming home, their precious new son between them. The wheels of the airplane left the ground and released the grip of despair from Kari's heart. At that same moment, she felt like the umbilical cord of her son's Cambodian life was cut. They were flying through the air together, as a family, ungrounded but whole

Ratanak with his new mom going home to Wyoming where he will become Eric Ratanak Grady Grossman (nicknamed Grady).

part two

A Child of the Khmer Rouge

"In spite of everything, I still believe that people are really good at heart."

Anne Frank

chapter six

The Irish Jewish Cambodian Cowboy

Kari smelled Cambodia as soon as she walked in the door of her home in Wyoming. The thick and tangy essence of coconut milk and curry accompanied a wave of sweet lime and galangal root, bridging her experience of Cambodia to her western American community. Amanda Prom and her mother had driven seventy miles from Lander, Wyoming, to bring a traditional Cambodian dish—*samla kh'tih satch moin* (yellow chicken curry)—to George and Kari's potluck baby shower in their home in Dubois.

While waiting for news of their adoption application, Kari had read about Amanda in a local newspaper article about her first trip back to Cambodia since escaping the war zone twenty years earlier. Kari had been excited to discover that her new son would not be the only Cambodian in Fremont County, Wyoming.

At the baby shower, Amanda gave Ratanak a golden necklace with an R on it, a traditional Cambodian charm meant to bring good luck and prosperity. Amanda's own baby jewelry had been cut up and sold in tiny increments before she turned ten; it had helped her family survive.

At the shower, George and Kari proudly announced the name they had given their new son: Grady. Kari kissed Grady's head and whispered his new name in his ear. She thought how her Irish surname didn't easily fit his little Asian face, but Grady responded readily to it. When combined with George's Jewish surname, Grossman, his proud new grandpa declared that Eric Ratanak Grady Grossman was an Irish, Jewish, Cambodian cowboy. His new name suited him just fine.

chapter seven

A Cambodian Wedding in Wyoming

As Kari and Amanda's friendship grew and strengthened, Kari and George decided to move their little family seventy miles from Dubois to Lander to be closer to Amanda and her family. Amanda had become a willing representative of the culture Grady had left behind. Kari hoped that living close to Amanda would help Grady grow up knowing the important parts of his Cambodian heritage and that it would give her the opportunity to learn about them as well.

As the families grew more and more comfortable with each other, Kari found herself spending more and more time at Amanda's restaurant, The China Garden, and of course, she brought Grady along. She enjoyed listening to the Cambodian language, called Khmer, though she didn't understand it. Khmer had a rhythm like a sputtering engine, alternating between guttural and nasal diphthongs, and punctuated by a rich medley of consonants such as bp, dt, and ch'ng. Eventually, Kari learned to pick out a few words, but mostly she enjoyed listening to the clucks and dips and high-pitched rises at the end of each sentence. She enjoyed hanging out with the "girls" and bonding over food, babies, and laughter, while Grady played and soaked up some of his culture through the language and good food.

On one occasion, Kari went to the restaurant and helped Amanda make Cambodian egg rolls—over four hundred of them. They gathered around a metal table in the storeroom and the lesson began. Kari's job was to peel back the thin sheets of dough, trying not to tear them, so they could be filled with a salad of shredded pork, cabbage, and carrot, which had been flavored with exotic spices and mild soy sauce. The egg rolls were for Amanda's youngest brother's wedding feast. Kari learned that the family would never serve their guests Chinese egg rolls, even though they ran the only Chinese restaurant in town. They're Cambodian; they don't eat Chinese food.

Most of the customers who pass through Amanda's restaurant mistakenly assume she's Chinese, despite the fact that she has a more circular face, full lips, round eyes, and curls in her jet-black hair—all characteristic of Southeast Asians. Kari thought it strange that an obvious difference such as skin color can dominate the more subtle details in another person's face, although most of the Cambodians she knows would say that all white folks look alike.

Around the metal table in the storeroom that day, Kari witnessed a sisterhood she had never known. For a moment, even though she was white on the outside, she felt brown on the inside, united with friends and family by the domestic chores of daily living.

Transracial families aren't exactly commonplace in Lander, Wyoming. Kari had become accustomed to curious looks when she took Grady with her on her errands around town. Most of the brown faces in Lander were Arapaho and Shoshone peoples from the nearby Wind River Indian Reservation. Sometimes Grady would be mistaken for American Indian. But in Amanda's restaurant, there was no mistaking his true heritage.

Suddenly Grady ran into the room and clutched at Kari's leg, trying to reach the goodies off the table. He loved egg rolls but hated fish sauce, much to her chagrin. Cambodians use fish sauce—a clear, brown liquid gathered from fermented salty fish after it's pressed—like table salt. It's also one of the reasons Amanda won't serve Cambodian food in her restaurant. Kari learned that you can't make Cambodian food without fish sauce, and fish sauce stinks! Amanda was afraid it would scare away customers.

Kari carefully broke off a piece of a hot fried egg roll, and Grady crawled into her lap to munch his treat. Meanwhile, large bowls of new ingredients were brought into the storeroom, and Amanda gave Kari meticulous instructions to make the perfect spring roll—another hand-rolled appetizer, fresh instead of fried.

Kari learned to layer rice noodles, fried pork, mint leaf, bean sprouts, and two small shrimps carefully onto a piece of wet rice paper, fold the edges around this pile of flavors, and shape it into a tidy envelope. Kari immediately dipped her first spring roll into the *tirk-trei* sauce and shoved it into her mouth. The tastes of sweetened fish sauce, garlic, and peanut mixed on her tongue, and she licked her fingers clean. She thought that she and Amanda were like two shrimps in a spring roll, wrapped together in their own little world, where the misery and mystery of Cambodia defined the border of both of their hearts.

Amanda's mother picked up Grady and tried to persuade him to eat some rice. He refused, closing his mouth and shaking his head. He was Cambodian on the outside, but Caucasian American on the inside, preferring macaroni and cheese to traditional Cambodian rice. George and Kari made a choice for him: family over culture. Kari hoped that once he was old enough to know his own mind, Grady would agree they had made the right decision.

Hot egg rolls returned from the fryer, and the pile of fresh spring rolls grew as well. More and more family members arrived for the wedding, greeting each other in rapid Khmer. Amanda's extended family was an impressive bunch: articulate, polite, and outgoing. Each sibling owned a Chinese restaurant in a rural western town. They had each stepped into rural America, mastered English, and left the trauma of war and genocide firmly buried in the past in order to prosper in the present.

As the wedding feast preparation continued, Kari realized just how much food was a part of the traditional Cambodian wedding rites, which can last three days or more. Usually the groom's family prepares half the food and the bride's family the other half. For this wedding, since the bride was a local Wyoming girl, Amanda's family made three or four traditional dishes while the bride's family contributed a buffet of sliced roast beef and potatoes. This blending of the two cultures gave Kari hope that one day she might be able to provide the same experience for her son.

During the wedding party and feast, someone asked Kari about Grady and how she had come to adopt him. While she was getting used to answering questions about her son, she would still ponder in her heart how she could raise a Cambodian child so far from his own culture and heritage. She knew that her son was born into the legacy of Pol Pot's killing fields, into a country rife with poverty and dysfunction. She knew that Grady had lost his birth family and culture, and he had gained her, George, and a new homeland filled with opportunity. But she still asked herself this question again and again: Does a parent's love make up for the loss of everything else?

Amanda's wedding to fellow Cambodian refugee Andy Ben in America, attended by her parents and friends who stood in for his parents because they had died in the war.

chapter eight

Amanda's Kitchen

Kari regularly brought Grady on her visits to the China Garden to cook with Amanda.

"*Sok sabai, kmouy?*" Amanda asked Grady when he and Kari met her at the kitchen door and removed their shoes in proper Asian fashion.

Grady hid between Kari's legs, too shy to answer the Khmer question, "How are you, nephew?" Kari asked Grady to *sompeah*, to bow with his hands together, to show respect toward Amanda. Respect for elders is a Cambodian value she felt Grady should know.

In the kitchen, Grandma, M'Yiey, was hunched over a bowl of long, green pods, the fruit of the tamarind tree. "You want to try?" She held one up, and Kari eagerly took one. A large bite caused her face to pucker. Amanda and her mother laughed at Kari's reaction and handed her a slice of fresh pineapple to combat the sourness. The sweet pineapple threw a punch too—a hot sting in the throat so painful it made her ears burn. It had been dipped in a paste of salt and hot chilies.

Amanda handed Kari a glass of water to drink once her coughing subsided, and she sipped it as she pounded her chest. Kari thought, "Half the reason they put up with my pestering to learn about Cambodia is that my stumbles over the Asian palate are so entertaining." She was continually surprised by the contrasts and extremes in Cambodian cooking.

"The Asian like hot and sour," Amanda said. "That's real Khmer food."

Real Khmer food is also a tender, loving expression that carries the weight of centuries. Food was, and still is, precious, cherished more than money or gold, desired through hunger pains, and made even more special by the longing for it. Cambodians use food to connect with each other.

Amanda stirred something in a pot on the stove. Kari looked in and saw a whole fish—head, bones, and all—in a soup. Amanda was making *sngow chruak trei* (sour fish soup), which makes Cambodian people feel at home, just as chicken noodle soup does for many Americans. Kari watched as Amanda peeled leaves from several small stems and tossed them into the pot.

"What's that?" she asked.

"Chi," Amanda replied.

"What's chi?"

"Herbs."

Each Cambodian cook makes up her own special blend of herbs that becomes her signature *chi* flavor, and Amanda wasn't about to tell Kari her secret ingredients.

When the soup was done, Kari and Grady stayed to eat. As Grady blew on his soup to cool it, Amanda touched his cheek and whispered, "Lucky, very lucky." Kari knew Amanda was remembering days when weak rice broth had done little to ease her own hunger pains. And while Kari didn't think that being abandoned in an orphanage, losing his birth parents, and being raised separately from his birth culture made Grady particularly lucky, she understood it was all a matter of perspective.

To understand the meaning of luck as Amanda knew it, Kari had to see the world through her eyes. One Sunday afternoon while teaching Kari how to grind peanuts and garlic into paste, Amanda began to recall her long-buried memories.

Kari and Amanda cooking in Amanda's kitchen.

chapter nine

Amanda's Childhood

It started with American bombs falling out of the sky when Amanda was three. At the time, she was known as Ponluethida Chen So Maly, but her family simply called her Maly. She began...

I was the fifth child born to Sokun Prom and Neang Om in Battambang, a city in the rice fields of northwest Cambodia. It was 1970, and a military general and the former prime minister, named Lon Nol, had just overthrown the Cambodian king. A civil war ensued with the King and Lon Nol fighting for power.

The United States decided to support Lon Nol with financial and military aid, believing that by helping him they could gain an ally in their fight with neighboring Vietnam. The king needed a bigger army to fight against Lon Nol and his US funding, so he chose to align himself with a small group of rebel fighters and former adversaries he called the Khmer Rouge.

As the war edged closer and closer to the eastern edge of the country, refugees fled into the western cities. This flood of refugees was a good thing for my family. We had a small roadside stand that sold snacks and dry goods. With the increasing population in the city, we were able to expand and buy a restaurant in Pailin.

Pailin was a resort city and a mining town because of the rare jewels found in the surrounding hills, and my early childhood was secure and safe there. Our restaurant was across the street from an expensive hotel, and my siblings and I would climb over the hotel wall and spy on the movie stars and other glamorous hotel guests. Like most children, I assumed that everyone lived the way I lived.

I looked up to my oldest brother, Dani, who was thirteen and could already speak French and read the newspaper. Dani and my other brother, Bon Leoun, who was eleven, lived in Battambang and ran our family's small dry-goods store with one of my cousins.

In April 1975, I was five years old and very excited about the approaching New Year's celebration because I knew my brothers would come home to Pailin for the three-day celebration. Our whole family would dress up in new clothes, go to the mountains together, feast, dance, and sing. It was the most exciting time of the year. I was proud that my father always wore a suit and talked to glamorous people in the restaurant. I heard the adults talk about Lon Nol and the king and the war, but I didn't know what it all meant.

As the New Year celebration ended, we were planning to say good-bye to my brothers the next day. I was helping my mom in the restaurant kitchen when I heard a commotion outside. I ran out the door to see what was happening. People were filling the streets, stopping traffic. Trucks pushed through the crowd with their horns blaring. Boys hung out of the back of the trucks, wielding guns with bayonets. They were all wearing what looked to me like black pajamas and red scarves. I thought maybe they were playing a soldier game.

In the streets, some people were waving Cambodian flags and cheering "Freedom Cambodia," but many were not smiling and cheering. A mixture of confusion and panic rippled through the crowd. One of the soldiers in black pajamas started yelling into a bullhorn. "Get out, everyone! You must go now! We must clean out the city. Take only food you can carry. You will return in three days." I didn't know whether to be thrilled or scared. I didn't understand what was happening.

My father started snapping orders to us, "Pack the food! Hide the pictures! Bury the jewelry!"

My mother quickly sewed all our gold baby jewelry into the waistband of her skirt. My brothers buried money and photographs into the ground behind the house, and my father stuffed paper money into cloth bags.

I did as I was told and piled into the neighbor's car along with the rest of my family and some of our neighbors. Then the car slowly muscled its way onto the street, into the throngs of people. It was crowded in the car, and I had to push myself up to see out the windows. I saw only unbelievable chaos. Everywhere people were running and yelling, some struggling to carry old people and young children. Some rode motos. Some pushed carts. Even patients from the hospital were walking the streets. The long line of humanity flowed on, as far as my eyes could see.

Armed men were directing traffic. "Go that way!" yelled a teenage soldier. "Angka wants you to go to the countryside!" I did not yet know what Angka meant but it appeared that Angka was the boss.

The boy soldiers spoke in a strange dialect and had no respect for their elders. My father appeared to understand perfectly, however, and he followed the boy's order without protest. I soon saw that complaints were met with a gun to the head. It was better to be quiet and follow orders.

chapter ten

The Long March
April 17, 1975

I saw and heard many terrible things that day. The Angka, which became known to the world as the Khmer Rouge, had "cleaned" the city by executing all the government officials and civilian workers loyal to Lon Nol. Before our car could reach the countryside, it was stopped by the soldiers and taken.

"Everyone must walk," a wild-eyed soldier shouted. "Angka will accept the car for revolutionary purposes."

Without protest, my father and our neighbor grabbed water, rice, and bags of money from the trunk, and we slipped into the crowd. Our families parted, wishing each other well with our eyes, since it was too dangerous to speak. The Angka soldiers led us all into the forest, following a dirt road that quickly diminished into a cow path. We walked and walked until our feet were sore and our legs exhausted. I had never been so tired and scared.

As darkness fell, we reached the rural village of Don Meay; there we set up a makeshift camp in a rice field. My mother prepared a quick meal of rice and fish, which we ate in silence, and then we fell into an exhausted sleep while soldiers patrolled among the campfires. I could see the firelight flickering on their guns as they walked among us.

The next day we walked again, thirteen kilometers (about eight miles), to the next town, without food or water. Hour after hour we walked. I lost track of how long we walked. We walked for days with little to eat or drink. We stopped in a small town called Rung and tried to buy food with our money, but we found out our money was no good anymore. Angka had outlawed money. It was worthless. So we used it for toilet paper or burned it in our fires. We survived by harvesting watercress from ponds we passed on our trek, but soon, everyone was sick.

The soldiers marched all of us to a large forested hill called Toul S'Nau and said, "You will make a new village here—a revolutionary activity!"

When the soldiers left, we took to the forest in search of food along with the thousands of refugees. My family and I scavenged food from the forest. With their bare hands, the boys caught squirrels, mice, snakes, and spiders. Whatever they found was boiled into a thin soup with salt and rationed among our nine family members. The most abundant wild fruit trees—banana, mango and sugar palm—were soon stripped bare.

Every day, the soldiers returned to oversee the building of the new village. With the onset of the rainy season, the river began to swell. Many started to worry that if we stayed in Toul S'Nau much longer, none of us would survive.

chapter eleven

The Year Zero

Our only source of information about what was happening in Cambodia came over a small radio, the station from Thailand secretly tuned into at night. Since the radio was so valuable, my mother was able to trade it to a nearby village chief in exchange for permission to build a small hut in his town, called Kampong Kohl. Finally, it seemed, my family was done walking.

The communist militants who had forced everyone to leave the city were known to the world as the Khmer Rouge, but I knew them only as Angka. *Angka* meant "the organization." It had a long list of new rules that we soon learned. Each day my parents and brothers went to the sugar cane fields to work, while my sisters and I went to a childcare group called the *go ma*. Old villagers were assigned to care for the refugee children, teach us revolutionary songs, and serve us one bowl of thin rice porridge per day. I quickly learned not to cry for more food, because when I did, I was hit with a bamboo switch until I stopped.

At daily meetings, the Khmer Rouge soldiers gave out the rules for Angka's new society. Money and education became the enemy, and all foreign influence was banned.

Jewelry, watches, and books were suspect. City dwellers were to plant and harvest the rice fields. Teachers, doctors, and nurses were ordered to "go to school" to teach the Angka soldiers their skills, but in reality, they were tortured, executed, and buried in mass graves.

My family and I took up rural forms of speech and gave each other country-sounding nicknames to hide our city-dweller past. I was so confused during this time that I stayed silent, keeping all my thoughts in my head. Words couldn't be spoken anyway, since no one knew whom to trust. We were quiet. Silence ate up most of our time.

Sometimes the soldiers would torture and kill people to make examples out of them. People were afraid to help each other for fear of drawing attention to themselves and their families. Everyone knew that to help would be a death sentence. Then I understood why my parents told me not to ask questions. Eat what they give you. Don't ask for more. It was, as Angka declared, the Year Zero. Everything from the past was gone; we lived in a new and unfamiliar society.

chapter twelve

Remembering Little Sister

Whipping around the bottom of a stainless-steel bowl, a beaten egg is tinted bright orange-yellow by the addition of finely ground turmeric root. Fistfuls of rice flour are added, and the batter begins to thicken to a foam. Coconut milk thins the mixture to the consistency of a thick soup. Amanda tosses in a pinch of salt and licks a finger to adjust the seasoning. Meanwhile, her mother stands at the counter, grinding pork into a fine meal and tossing it into a hot wok perched over the flaming cauldron of an industrial-size, Asian-style kitchen. It's Sunday, Amanda's only day off, and the cooking lessons for Kari continue.

As the pork browns, julienned strips of onion are added and a ladle of batter is spread quickly over a hot, flat pan. Timing is everything. The easy, rhythmic movements of mother and daughter are like a dance. When the batter is about to reach pancake consistency, Amanda tosses in a couple of spoonfuls of cooked pork and bean sprouts. A minute later, one side of the circle is folded over the other, omelet style, and it's slid with ease onto a ceramic plate. Amanda hands the plate to Kari.

"*Ban Cheow*, you call Half-moon Cake," she says. "That's the one my sister ask for before she die."

Amanda continues her story...

There are no pictures of my little sister, Srey Pau; she exists only in our memories. I remember a skinny little girl who complained too much, refused to follow directions, and incessantly demanded to wear pretty things. She was what you call a "girly girl." I think she was just a perfectly normal three-year-old whose contrary nature intensified as she began to starve in Kampong Kohl.

In the mornings, I would sometimes hear my family members waking in the dark. Nine of us lived in a single room about three square meters (nine square feet) and raised off the ground on small wooden stilts. We were always quiet. Through the palm thatch wall, I could hear the family in the next hut shuffling about, and they never talked either. No one did, because outside the sleeping quarters, chhlops were always lurking.

Chhlops were peasant boys, usually nine or ten years old, sent to spy and then tell the Angka leaders everything they saw and heard. They embraced the task with enthusiasm. It was their job to be mean, and they were rewarded for it. Their payment for spying was food and power. Seeking the rewards of that power, they would embellish their stories to gain the favor of their Angka big brothers. We all hated them, and it drove me crazy living in fear of them, listening for their footsteps under our floorboards. It was safer to be quiet.

One morning I gazed at my mother in the early dawn light, and I noticed that her face was getting darker and darker from the months of hard work in the fields. I tried to imagine my beautiful mother chopping vegetables and stirring noodles in our restaurant's kitchen. I could barely remember those happy times, and the thought of food was now painful. We were always so hungry.

My mother picked up the sleeping baby, Atuit, and tied him into her *krama*, a traditional cloth she used as a baby sling, tightly bound to her back. I could see Atuit's shoulder bones and ribs outlined through the thin fabric of the krama. I rolled onto my back and examined my own skinny arms. I looked full though, the skin stretched tight over my extended belly. I wondered, why does my stomach look so full when I am so hungry?

Srey Pau was still asleep when my mother and Atuit slipped out the door to join the women's work brigade, walking in long lines toward another hopeless, hot day in the sugarcane field. It was better to be gone before my baby sister woke up and started to complain, because the chhlops were always listening.

That night I learned that I no longer lived in Cambodia. At our nightly group meeting in the center of the compound, the Angka leaders were shouting out that we now lived in Democratic Kampuchea. The leader was angry with us for our poor food production for the new country. He ranted about the proper care of sugarcane and proper harvesting.

He yelled, "Today we work late in the moonlight instead of sleep. Why? Because you did not finish one hectare! Do not say the soil is too hard. We will not listen to your complaints. You must sacrifice for Angka!"

The crowd raised their tired fists and repeated, "Che'yo Angka! Che'yo," a chant for the victory of Angka, My brother Dani pumped his fist and rolled his eyes at me, making me laugh.

"Where is all this food going?" I whispered to him.

"Always more and more," Dani whispered back. "They work us like machines, but we never go to take care of what is at the back. Sugarcane grows all year. We just can't plant more. We must harvest too."

The economy of Democratic Kampuchea was flawed from the start. What was not used to feed the Angka leaders and soldiers was traded to China in exchange for weapons. Failure to produce the quota was easier to blame on the workers' lack of revolutionary spirit than on the new government's flawed organization.

The meeting dragged on late into the night, and the next morning I felt droopy and tired with just a few hours of poor sleep. As soon as I woke up, I was aware of my empty belly, so I woke up Srey Pau and we walked outside for our morning ritual to get ready for *go ma*. All the children left in the camp stood in perfectly straight lines, each with our hand on the shoulder of the child in front of us. We would sing the new national anthem:

The red, red blood splatters the cities and plains of the Cambodian fatherland,
The sublime blood of the workers and peasants.
The blood of revolutionary combatants of both sexes.
The blood spills out into great indignation and a resolute urge to fight,
17 April, that day under the revolutionary flag,
The blood certainly liberates us from slavery.

Then we would all march to the communal kitchen where Mit Bong, "Comrade Big Sister," would serve us breakfast. Every morning we were given a bowl of water with a few rice grains floating in it. Seeing it, I felt the strong urge to start screaming, but my big sister Malis pulled at my sleeve and shook her head. I calmed down, and we sat down outside to eat.

I handed my bowl to Srey Pau, who grabbed it and poured the contents into her mouth. I thought maybe my mother, out working in the fields, would be able to bring home some insects for us to eat that night. The idea was so comforting that I was glad I hadn't complained about breakfast; I had learned to avoid being hit by the bamboo switch.

Sure enough, my mother did bring home a tasty morsel for me that night. As she padded along the soft ground in the fields, she would plant small sections of sugar cane and pack loose dirt around the little green shoot. When the chhlops weren't looking, she'd quickly stick one end of the sugar cane in her mouth and bite down, sucking the juice out as fast as she could. She had just planted a shoot when a scorpion appeared from behind the furrow. With a quick whip of her krama, she killed it and shoved it into her pocket. She knew any nutritious morsel would bring a smile to one of her children's faces.

Late that afternoon, when she returned from the fields, Mother pulled the scorpion from her pocket and gave it to me. I grabbed it, pulled off the stinger, and ate it raw. I was so grateful! I really wanted to hug my mother. I wanted to kiss her and thank her. But I couldn't. We had been living under Angka law for almost a year, and I knew the rules. You never knew when a chhlop might be watching.

Srey Pau didn't understand why we were so quiet and cautious. She was too young to make sense of everything that had happened. When Mother came home from the fields each night, Srey Pau would cry, "Mai! Mai! Hungry! Want *ban cheow*!" and twist her skinny arms and legs around Mother's waist.

"No, no, don't have," she would scold. "Shh! Don't call me Mai!"

"Why don't call you Mai?" Srey Pau would protest, scowling. She had been told a hundred times not to use the city-dweller word for Mommy, because if the chhlops heard that word they might report it to the Angka.

"I want pretty clothes. I want a necklace. I want *ban cheow*!" She would scream and cry, and it would turn into a full-blown temper tantrum.

As she grew more irate, neighbors tried to help. Angka called them "old people," which meant a family who had lived in the rural village, farming the land for many generations. While the minds of the "old people" in Kampong Kohl may not have been "corrupted" by city life, neither had the Angka's vengeful spirit consumed their hearts. Hearing the cries of a little girl from a family who worked hard and minded their own business, they reached out to help little Srey Pau.

The lady next door would hold Srey Pau on the steps of her hut, swaying back and forth, saying, "Shh! Shh! Why are you crying, Pau?" Sometimes the old woman would cry too.

Fried red ants are a Cambodian delicacy. During the war, Maly searched for them in trees and ate them raw to stay alive. The white part is the egg sacks; she liked that part best.

chapter thirteen

Half-Moon Cake

A childless couple living in a wooden house across the dirt alley went to work gathering the ingredients for *ban cheow*. Turmeric root grew in the forest surrounding the village, so that was easy to find. Someone shimmied up a coconut tree to get milk for the bowl, while others stole an egg from a duck that nested on the dyke. The women quickly pounded some rice into flour. No one had pork to make the filling, but bean sprouts grew in the family garden; old people were still allowed to harvest their own gardens privately. In no time, the quiet neighbors in Kampong Kohl returned with some half-moon cake to quiet Srey Pau as well as a little bit for the rest of the family.

I thought that nothing had ever tasted so good as that sliver of half-moon cake! I licked my fingers to make sure every last morsel was eaten. It had literally been weeks since I'd eaten real food.

"Food, look, food, Mai!" Srey Pau beamed. "I like it." She ate and ate and ate. The old people smiled.

But then the begging resumed. "Mai, I want a necklace."

Srey Pau babbled about a necklace and earrings while pulling at my mother's clothes. What if she were to give away what was hidden in the seams of Mother's sarong? Tiny golden necklaces, anklets, and earrings—the hidden jewels were totems of good luck and prosperity purchased at the time of each child's birth and blessed at the temple.

A bolt of blue *pamoung* silk was stashed between the rafter and our roof thatch. Mai cut a small piece from it, wrapped it around Srey Pau's puffed-out belly, and tucked the ends through her tiny legs, tying them into a *kben*, the traditional dancer's pantaloon. Mai hoped the bright material would finally calm her.

"Pretty, pretty!" Srey Pau was delighted, but it wasn't enough. "I want a necklace!" she screamed.

I wondered why she wanted to look pretty. I looked down at my own soiled, black trousers, and I got a little angry that Mai would spoil my little sister so much. But I was so happy that I got to share some of the half-moon cake that I didn't complain out loud. I just thought, "My sister has such a big mouth. She's going to get us into trouble!"

Finally, my mother unbound a small, gold earring from the bottom seam of her sarong, hoping the risk would be worth it if it finally quieted Srey Pau. It did the trick. Between sniffles and tears, she finally fell into an exhausted sleep. In her fancy clothes with a tummy full of *ban cheow*, Srey Pau finally gave up. She drifted off, never to return. Starvation took her that night.

When she did not awaken in the morning, my family mourned in silence. Someone fetched a monk to say a blessing over her small body. Before Angka, a funeral would call forth the ancestors to escort Srey Pau to the other side, but the monk couldn't go with us to the funeral hill, because it was too dangerous. He made a quick blessing over her body and wrapped it in plain cloth.

My father said quiet prayers while he carried her to the chosen gravesite. Two neighbors followed to help dig the hole. My mother joined the women's work brigade with Atuit on her back, tears falling silently onto the krama wrap. My brothers went to the fields. Malis and I walked slowly to *go ma*. No one even noticed that Srey Pau was gone.

I sat in the dirt all day, throwing stones. I didn't know if I was happy or sad. My sister had died, so I didn't have to listen to her constant complaining, but her complaining had gotten half-moon cake for us all the day before. When I think of it now, I cry tears of guilt because that's how I felt at the time. But I was *so* hungry.

Two days later, the old woman next door died too. To honor her, her relatives rounded up a funeral feast in the customary fashion. From the forest around the village, they harvested deer meat and palm juice, raccoon, and rabbit. The chhlops who came were her kin, so we didn't worry so much about spies in the company of mourners.

For a moment, no one seemed to care about the repercussions, and we lived in the traditional world that made sense. My family and I ate our fill at the funeral. I was so happy! I couldn't wait for the next person to die, so I could eat. That's how hungry we were then.

One week after Srey Pau died, little Atuit died in his sleep as well. His last request—one of the only words he knew at only eighteen months of age—was *nom ba chok* (rice noodle curry). It was the last meal we had eaten together as a family for the New Year celebration at our home in Pailin. But for Atuit, there was no blessing, no mourning, no feast, and no funeral. That's just the way it was.

* * * * *

Kari, Amanda, and Grandma sat quietly in the kitchen when Amanda finished her story.

Grandma said with tears streaming down her cheeks, "I think my daughter Srey Pau die to help my family." She spooned fish sauce over Kari's half-moon cake, and then she stopped and held Kari's hand as if she were touching the ghosts of her lost daughter and son. "I think she traded her life for our family. That's why we can get a job and stay in Kampong Kohl. If she not die, maybe my whole family die."

Grandma's eyes looked deep into Kari's. In her pained expression, Kari imagined she could see into the heart of Grady's birth mother, and she thought, "In motherhood, we are all one."

Prom family and other members of the Cambodian refugee community in Denver, Colorado 1987. Amanda is in the front row, about 15 years old.

chapter fourteen

Daikon Camp

"My family and I learned how to survive under the Angka rule," Amanda said to Kari the next time they cooked. Then she described how they survived, eventually escaped from Kampuchea, and made their way to the United States.

My older sister, Malis, and I were taken away from our family in Kampong Kohl and placed in Daikon Camp. Mit Bong told us we would learn to read and write and work for Angka. Our brothers were sent off to work in teenage work camps. We didn't know where they were or if they were still alive. I ran away once in the night and discovered that our parents were still alive and still living in our old village but it had been months since we had seen any of our family.

Mit Bong lied. There was no reading and writing at the children's collective camp, just sandy fields to plant and wild monkeys waiting in the trees to bite us. Each night Malis and I slept side-by-side on a wooden plank floor in a row with several hundred girls our age. There was a large, metal roof over our heads to protect us from the rain, but we were defenseless against the mosquitoes.

Each morning began the same. We assembled into perfectly straight lines in front of the long house, hands to shoulders, waiting to be inspected. Young Angka guards walked up and down the rows, watching ruthlessly for defiant behavior, wielding their power. After the inspection, we marched to the fields, where we planted daikon seeds.

The sand was hot; it burned our bare feet. We worked fast to avoid being hit by the guards. We were hungry all the time, and the heat made us dizzy. While I filled buckets with water from the river to pour over the new seeds, I watched the ground for any edible morsel—lizard, insects, snails, or even daikon root.

One night I lay nervously beside Malis, feeling overwhelmed by hunger. I couldn't stop thinking about all the daikon root we had spent the afternoon splitting, just lying up there on our metal roof, drying. It was more than I could bear! I got up, careful not to wake any of the sleeping girls around me. I slipped down the steps and then circled back to the far end of the building. I shimmied up the roof post and made my way across the roof, shoving daikon roots into my krama cloth while sticking one in my mouth to chew. When the cloth was full, I got down and buried most of the roots under a nearby bush. Then I snuck back to my sleeping place and waited, my heart pounding, for someone to discover what I'd done and come get me.

Nothing happened. I woke my sister and gave her a piece of the root to eat. "Give me your krama," I whispered, "I want to go see Ma."

"No, they'll kill you," she said.

"I don't care." My adrenaline was running high. "I can take food and rabbit poop to her." Rabbit poop was what we called the little rolled pellets of charcoal the Angka used for medicine to treat dysentery.

I crept quietly through the forest at the edge of the daikon fields. The journey felt like hours as I walked and ran, guided by my internal navigation system that recognized familiar trees and bushes. When I finally reached Kampong Kohl, I snuck quietly behind the palm thatch huts until I found the one where I used to live.

I crept up the steps of the hut and spied a row of large banana leaves covering a small hole in the floor. Inside I found several stalks of sugarcane. I stuffed the sugarcane in my krama and left the daikon root in its place so my mother would know I'd been there. I made my way back to my camp. I did this every now and then—sneaking away in the night to exchange food with my mother. This way, we both knew the other was alive.

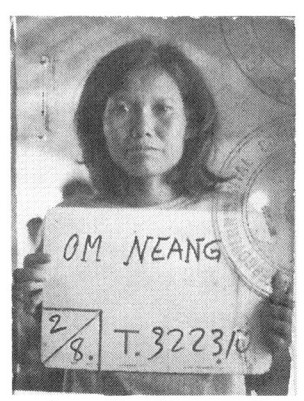

Amanda's mother, Om Neang, in a refugee photo from Khau I Dang refugee camp in Thailand.

Amanda's father, Prom Sokun, in a refugee photo from Khau I Dang refugee camp in Thailand.

chapter fifteen

Escape

Three years had passed. My parents were in Kampong Kohl; Malis and I worked in the daikon camp; and my brothers were in a teenage work camp. But we were all still alive. Things were changing, though. Provoked by Pol Pot's arrogance at starting renewed border disputes, Vietnam invaded Cambodia in January of 1979. And suddenly word spread through the daikon camp that the Vietnamese were coming. I didn't know if they would be friends or enemies, so I grabbed Malis and we ran. We ran as fast as we could to find our mother.

The front lines moved quickly across the country. In the chaos of the Vietnamese advance and the Khmer Rouge retreat, all the work camps were liberated, and the workers took to the roads and footpaths in search of their families. I had made the journey to Kampong Kohl so many times in the dark that I knew the way by heart, so I pushed my way through the people with Malis behind me.

We arrived at Kampong Kohl late in the afternoon and met up with our parents. Angka told everyone to evacuate the village, but my brothers weren't with us yet, so we didn't want to leave. My father decided to defy

Angka's orders, and we hid in a cave that night. We could hear the Angka soldiers killing all the families that had not left as ordered. We were so scared. It was a terrible, long night.

In the morning, my father left to search for my brothers. The village was eerily empty, and we could hear fighting as the Vietnamese army approached. Mother, Malis, and I waited in that cave for two days. When we were about to give up all hope and leave, my father appeared with my three brothers. We were so happy to see each other, but we didn't know what to say, because it had been so long since we'd all been together.

To escape Angka, we ran toward the river and hid by the banks along with hundreds of other refugees. We all crouched down and waited for the gunfire from the fighting to stop. But the fighting went on for hours. Malis and I clung to each other, steeling ourselves against the piercing reports of gunfire over our heads.

By the time the morning fog had cleared, the Angka were in retreat. We saw our chance, and there was a panicked surge for the river. Everyone ran fast and jumped into the water, hundreds of people. We didn't look back. We just kept running until nighttime.

That night, my family found ourselves walking on the road with a column of Vietnamese trucks and tanks. The road was noisy with chickens and cows, people screaming and crying, all kinds of panic. We were scared to get off the road and go into the forest because of the many landmines. One day someone found a grenade and tossed it into a pond. When it exploded, we all went in and grabbed the dead fish floating to the surface to eat for dinner that night.

We reached our old home in Battambang a few days later, but nothing was left except for foundation and some wooden beams. We set up a makeshift camp there and scavenged for food and shelter. My mother still had some of her gold jewelry, which my father managed to trade for food and a little Thai money. My brothers scavenged in the forest, hoping not to step on the landmines buried there.

Six weeks after we were liberated from the camps, my father decided it was time to leave Cambodia. We walked through a landmine-infested forest to Thailand. My mother was seven months pregnant at the time.

When we got across the border into Thailand, we were loaded onto buses and driven a few miles down the road to a United Nations refugee camp. Hundreds of skinny Khmers filed off the buses and into the registration lines. Relief workers scurried among us. I thought they looked like giants compared to us!

When I reached the front of the line, I felt mesmerized by the woman who asked me my name. She had freckled white skin, blue eyes, and an amazing, sweet smell. She was the most astonishing person I had ever seen. She offered me an apple, and I grabbed it, taking a bite quickly because I thought she might change her mind and take it away. For the first time in many years, I felt my tension release, and I thought, "Maybe I'm safe now."

chapter sixteen

Refugee

My family was given a five-by-five-meter (sixteen-by-sixteen-foot) piece of plastic and a small pile of bamboo to use to build our new home in the Khau I Dang refugee camp. We were also issued a stipend of food: salt-dried fish, dry milk, rice, and cabbage. It wasn't a lot, but it was more than we'd had in such a long time that we felt lucky.

On the advice of some of the other refugees, my father got to work writing letters to every country open to accepting Cambodian exiles. He wrote letter after letter to France, Australia, and the United States. We waited two years in the refugee camp for a reply.

In the meantime, we all worked hard to earn food and money. My brothers, Dani and Bon Leoun, set their sights on learning English. They couldn't afford a place in the crowded private-school classroom, so they stood quietly outside the open-air windows and listened, copying down every word the teacher wrote on the chalkboard. In just a few months, Dani mastered English well enough to translate for the new refugees in the camp hospital. My father's experience running his business earned him a place as quartermaster for the United Nations. He was in charge of the school supplies in camp.

At least once every day, we walked to the camp post office and scanned the list of names on the big, white sponsorship board to see if our family would be one of the lucky ones approved to move to a friendly country. "Please give us a superpower country," I prayed, "but not a communist one!" Daily disappointment was beginning to erode our dreams of freedom.

One evening my father came home and announced we had a sponsor! He was a military policeman from Battambang who used to be a regular customer in our restaurant. Somehow, one of our letters had reached him in a place called Denver, Colorado. The letter from the United States hung like gold in the air; there was no containing our excitement!

For the next two months, we traveled through transit camps until we finally made it to Chunbari, where we boarded a 747 airplane. "The airplane is on the sky," I whispered. It was the only English phrase I knew.

We flew to the Philippines and spent six months there learning how to function in a modern world. It was 1982, and I was twelve years old. I saw my first telephones, flush toilets, television, traffic lights, electricity, and running water. Everything was new and startling. In the Philippines we had food and freedom, and I could finally be a child again. I could breathe deep and laugh hard. We lived in a two-room concrete block apartment with a hard roof and a floor. We had a lush, green creek to play in, and I attended school—complete with books and a television. I couldn't imagine that America could be any better than that!

In September of 1982, we made the last leg of our journey and stepped onto American soil at the Stapleton International Airport in Denver. Cambodians, including our old friend, Rasmey, from Battambang, greeted us. I looked at his healthy, plump family and wondered, "How come they're not skinny like us?" We headed toward the looming mountains for our first meal in America.

When we first got here we were so poor, we didn't have one dime to our name. And we didn't know how to do anything at all. We wanted American-sounding names, and I chose Amanda.

Mastering English was the first order of business, and the whole family started attending a special class called ESL (English as a Second Language). My mother found a job cleaning at a nursing home, and my father became a janitor there. By the end of the summer, we had saved a thousand dollars and were able to pay off our debt to Catholic Charities, which had paid our airfare to the United States.

That night my father announced to us that he didn't want us to depend on the government any longer. By this time, my parents had learned enough English to get better jobs cutting glass at a window factory. My brothers worked as janitors at the school, and Malis and I babysat our new baby brother, who had been born in the refugee camp. In our spare time, we collected cans from dumpsters on our block to trade for dimes to spend at the local Salvation Army store.

A few years later, with the help of a Chinese moneylender, my father was able to open our first family restaurant in Mitchell, South Dakota. Fifteen years earlier, we had been driven out of our family restaurant in Pailin. I started waiting tables there and married my husband, Punthea Rith.

When my father announced he had found a fixer-upper called China Garden in Lander, my husband and I decided it was time we made our own way. Now that China Garden is a success, I can give back to others. Now

I can make yearly trips back to Cambodia. I visit random villages, helping them drill wells for drinking water.

* * * * * *

Amanda finished her story, and Kari thought about fate—her own and Amanda's—drawing together in Wyoming. It was the first time Kari really understood what the American Dream means.

Amanda's refugee photo from Khau I Dang refugee camp in Thailand.

part three

Teacher Absent Often

*"Although the world is full of suffering,
it is also full of the overcoming of suffering."*

Helen Keller

chapter seventeen

Building a School

Even before their adoption trip, before spending hours with Sovann on his moto in Phnom Penh and learning Amanda's story in her kitchen, George and Kari were bothered by the thought of leaving Cambodia with a baby and not doing something for the children left behind. They decided that as part of their adoption commitment, they needed to help Cambodia's children through education. At the time, rural Cambodia had almost no schools, and most rural children either didn't go to school or studied for a year or two on a dirt patch out in the open or perhaps under a tree. Kari and George decided they wanted to build a school in their new son's honor.

For several months before their adoption trip to Cambodia, Kari had been researching and raising money by selling photographs of the Rocky Mountains over the Internet to family, friends, and colleagues; she succeeded in raising fifteen thousand dollars to donate to American Assistance for Cambodia (AAC), an organization with an ambitious goal to build two hundred rural schools.

While in Cambodia, one of the stops on Sovann's moto tour of Phnom Penh had been the AAC office. On the office wall was a map of Cambodia with thumbtacks placed where they had already built schools. Kari pointed to an area on the map with no thumbtacks to choose the location for the Grady Grossman School. Their school would be number eighty-one. The place was Chrauk Tiek village in the Cardamom Mountains near Mount Aural, the highest mountain in Cambodia. They thought this location would be a perfect match for a family from Wyoming that loved mountains.

George and Kari asked Sovann to visit Chrauk Tiek with them and he agreed to help. They rented a Land Cruiser for the six-hour journey. The dusty, pot-holed road took them west of Phnom Penh and then north from the town of Kampong Speu toward the forest-covered hills in the misty distance. The long, bumpy ride was made even more difficult by the lack of a bridge at four shallow river crossings.

When they reached the small village, they visited the primary school, which was a dilapidated hut with no walls, a dirt floor, and huge holes in the thatch roof. Fifty children sat shoulder-to-shoulder on logs, sharing a few newsprint books. Three teachers passed a single piece of chalk between them, writing lessons on wooden boards they had painted black and nailed to a post. Looking up at the gaping holes in the roof, Kari asked what they did during the rainy season. One teacher answered, "No school."

George and Kari spent the afternoon talking to the children, with Sovann helping to interpret. "What do you want to be when you grow up?" seemed such a stupid question in a world with so little choice, but they asked it anyway. With some coaching by Sovann, a few of the children tentatively stood up one at a time and answered. Almost every one of them wanted to be a teacher. Two or three wanted to be a doctor or nurse. No one said they wanted to be farmers, which is what all their parents were. Kari told the children that if they would come to school, she and George would make sure they had what they needed to learn, and the first item of business would be to build a real school.

Before they left the dusty schoolyard that first day, one dirty girl in a mismatched green shirt and sarong (skirt) stepped slowly forward. Staring at Kari in an unconvinced but inquisitive way, she put her hands together and bowed. Kari thought this little girl hadn't believed her words but that she had hope.

A new building site had already been selected by the village leaders a few kilometers back toward the village, on the bank of the Kantout River, where a pile of concrete blocks were stacked and waiting. American Assistance planned to install a rooftop solar panel on the new building; it would power a computer they hoped might introduce the children to basic technology. But the children didn't have shoes, uniforms, books, or school supplies. A building would be just the beginning.

Back in Phnom Penh, Sovann took George and Kari to a bank so they could set up an account to transfer money from the United States to Cambodia to fund projects at the school on their own. Sovann had never used a bank, so they donated the initial one hundred dollars to open an account in his name. As George instructed Sovann on how to fill out the forms, his lips started to twitch, then he started to pace, and soon perspiration rolled from his forehead, even in the cool, air-conditioned lobby. "What if the bank close, and the government throw away the money?" he stammered.

No matter how hard George tried to explain the business of banking to him, the boy in Sovann couldn't release his adult body from haunting memories. Sovann was only seven years old when the Khmer Rouge army had marched into Phnom Penh and forcibly evacuated hundreds of thousands of the city's inhabitants, closing all the banks and abolishing money. As Sovann walked out of the city with his widowed mother, four sisters, and little brother toward the countryside and more than a decade of poverty and starvation, the useless currency was blowing in the streets. From that day forward, no matter how hard he worked or how much money he saved, Sovann would never feel secure. This legacy of fear and distrust was what George and Kari hoped their school could change for the children in Chrauk Tiek.

The Grady Grossman School opened in 2001. It's in the southern Cardamom Mountains at the edge of the Aural Wildlife Sanctuary, a biological World Heritage site designated for protection in 1997. At the time the Khmer Rouge regime ended, this forest had the most diverse species of flora and fauna in Southeast Asia. Aural Mountain is Cambodia's highest peak—1,700 meters of endangered old-growth tumloap trees and one of the last remaining habitats for Asian tigers, clouded leopards, sun bear, gibbons, and tree sloths. It would soon become ground zero for the environmental destruction and corruption that would tear the village apart. And the school would become a lightning rod, empowering the villagers to change things.

chapter eighteen

"Teacher Absent Often"

Kari and George didn't realize when they donated the money to build their school that the agreement to run the school between American Assistance and the Cambodian government was flawed. If the Cambodian government didn't have the money to run the school before it was built, what made anyone think that it could run it afterward?

As Grady grew from baby to toddler to kindergartner in Wyoming, each year Kari left him home with George and returned to Cambodia to check on the school. She asked a lot of questions, and the answers always bothered her. With a new building, the attendance at the Grady Grossman School tripled to 150 children in grades one to six, ranging in age from six to sixteen. However, starting in about third grade half the class would drop out each year, and by the time they reached sixth grade, almost 80 percent of the students had dropped out. Only 10 percent went on to attend seventh grade at the middle school down the road, few of them girls. A handful of boys finished middle school, and none went to high school.

Government teachers were only paid thirty dollars per month, which wasn't enough to live on. Teachers often didn't show up, were late or drunk, or took long, lazy breaks, putting in just enough effort to collect their pittance of a salary. One teacher even had a barber chair set up outside the classroom; if someone came for a haircut, the class had to wait.

Since the Chrauk Tiek community was illiterate, teachers from as far away as Kampong Speu, sixty kilometers to the south, were assigned to this remote village, but they had no housing, no food, no bathroom, no clean water, no transportation, and no family or rice field nearby to cultivate. They had to catch bugs and frogs to survive. Teachers often went home to their families for food and didn't return for weeks on end. Teacher absenteeism caused students to drop out.

Kari continued to raise money by selling Cambodian silk crafts each Christmas and then visiting the school with Sovann each spring to spend the money on whatever the school needed to keep functioning. The most obvious problems were fixed first. The teachers needed shelter, so she gave Sovann four thousand dollars to buy wood panels, cement, and tin roofing, and to hire carpenters to build a five-room teacher residence. With the addition of an outhouse-style bathroom, complete with a tiled floor and river-water cistern for bathing, the six teachers were the envy of the entire school district. It was the first bathroom they'd ever had. Every month Sovann delivered a food stipend of rice, dried fish, and sour soup mix to the teachers.

The cheaply dug well and water pump broke the first year in operation, so Kari had the well dug deeper and replaced the pump with a good German model. She learned that it's customary for hired Cambodians to use the cheapest materials available for humanitarian aid projects so they could pocket as much cash as possible while still appearing to get the job done.

Once the teachers' residence was built, student attendance soared to over three hundred students. Kari stayed in the shelter herself and spent weeks living in Chrauk Tiek among the villagers with no electricity or running water. She got to know the principal, the teachers, and the parents. She learned that when children graduate from grade six, they have two possible futures in Chrauk Tiek: work in the rice fields and barely subsist, or cut down trees, destroying their future in the process, for a monthly wage that's five times greater than a teacher's salary.

Half of the students in the Grady Grossman School were children of illegal loggers. Their fathers were typically illiterate, demobilized soldiers who had been stolen as teenagers and put into the army by force. With no other opportunity for work, they followed their former commanders, felling trees and loading whole tree trunks onto oxcarts, then driving them to market through the night for two dollars. At night, fewer bribes needed to be paid to police officers, military police, and anyone else with political power along the route, so the poorest oxcart drivers transported their contraband at night. The endless parade of huge hardwood trees down the road were headed for Vietnam and China, where they were fashioned into luxury furniture to be sold in cities in Asia, Europe, and America. Kari hoped the school would prosper and bring more awareness about illegal logging in the area.

The other half of the students were the children of Souy villagers. The Souy are a minority tribe of forest dwellers who have lived in the mountains for centuries.

They often gather edible plants from the forest, because when they farm rice, it provides only enough food for three to six months. They often go hungry. Many people make less than one dollar a day selling cooking sticks or charcoal. Their families are large, with eight to fourteen children, and usually half of them die for lack of food and medicine. The Souy believe their ancestors' spirits dwell in tall, old trees. Their culture is tied to the forest as a source of food and medicine. When the forest dies, the Souy culture will die with it.

Every time Kari went back to Cambodia, she passed a newly built school that stood empty. She decided to go visit some of these abandoned schools and see what was going on. In a village called Sre Chrap, two kilometers (about a mile) deep in the forest near Chrauk Tiek, she met school-age children driving cattle, operating chainsaws, and carrying babies. Girls dropped out of school so they could be married off at fifteen and start having babies, beginning the cycle of poverty all over again. She asked why they weren't in school, and the answer was always the same: "teacher absent often."

More than a hundred school-age children in the three surrounding villages didn't go to school, but not for lack of a building. The village had a nice, bright yellow, three-classroom building carved out of the forest and built by Lutheran World Services in 2001. A mother with five children and a baby squatted in the shade of a tree outside the school. Her oldest boy, Hong, age ten, was holding a rope for driving cattle. Kari asked the mother why he wasn't in school. She said he had dropped out two years before, because "teacher absent often."

For such families, sending a child to school is a huge sacrifice; keeping their children out of school is a matter of survival. They also give up on education quickly if they see no hope in it. Can you blame them? Hong walked a long way to go to school, and his mother needed his labor to help feed the family. What treasures of talent lay behind Hong's bright eyes, buried forever because no one could be bothered to pay a teacher to mine it? The story was the same in hut after hut.

In the Sre Chrap schoolyard, Kari met the principal and four villagers. They had built a fence to keep out the cows and wanted to build a teacher house, but they needed ten bags of cement for the floor and tin for the roof. She was impressed with what they'd accomplished and approved their request. Building fences and buildings is something illiterate people can do very well. Kari asked the villagers what they could do to support qualified teachers to stay there. The answer was simple: provide them housing, clean water, and a salary. But how could they support teachers with a living wage if no one in the village had a job with a salary?

Two "community teachers" taught the sixty students in the school that day; the woman teaching first grade had a fourth-grade education; and the man teaching second grade had an eighth-grade education. A handful of third- and fourth-graders learned from the principal, who was the only high school graduate trained to be a teacher. There were no students in fifth or sixth grade.

Four kilometers in the opposite direction, Kari visited a school where twenty-six-year-old Hong Bun Han was teaching third grade. He had completed tenth grade himself but had no teacher training. Kari asked the forty kids in his class how many of them attended school often, and only five raised their hands. In the next classroom, forty-two fourth-graders were hanging out. "Where's the teacher?" Kari asked. They pointed to the door, where

Hong Bun Han was standing. He was the teacher for both classes!

Two classrooms had no teacher at all. Of the eight students in the sixth grade, all four sixteen-year-old girls said they wanted to be teachers. Three of the fifteen-year-old boys said the same thing. One boy wanted to be a doctor. Their school had an abandoned solar panel on the roof, an inoperable computer in the corner, and a broken well. The once large "victory garden" was now a dried-up field; the gardener left when the donor did.

"Donated by George Mrus" was painted on the end of the building. Kari wondered if Mr. Mrus knew about what was happening at the school. The staff at American Assistance told her he had gotten "donor fatigue." She was beginning to see the problem with donor-driven projects; they last only as long as the donor does.

Kari realized she was doing the same thing as the donors at the other schools. She was sending a rice stipend every month, buying school supplies, and supplying teacher housing. There were already over three hundred children depending on her and growing. If she stopped, the school would probably be abandoned. Kari realized that she needed to find a way to make her school and the surrounding schools able to support themselves, so after the donors built the schools and left, the community could keep the school going on their own.

George and Kari adopted a daughter, Shanti, from India in 2006, so that year Kari couldn't visit Chrauk Tiek. Shanti was two years old, and it wasn't a good idea to leave her during the critical first year of bonding to her new parents. Shanti had a rough start in life, and Kari wanted to be with her. Shanti was now three and had to stay home with George and Grady while her new mom was away. Kari started to wonder, "What if I don't come back?"

Kari visited the next village, where the story was the same: two buildings, one built by American Assistance, and the other—bright yellow and newly built by Lutheran World Services—made for a total of ten empty classrooms. Why would they build a second building when they couldn't run the first one? From the sign on the building, Kari gathered that the "Lutheran Education Fund of the Adelaide Hills, Australia" needed a capital project. Mission accomplished. School built. Pity no students were in it.

Toward the end of her visit in January 2007, Kari made a point to visit the village of Bonteay Pranak, which had the only secondary school (grades seven through nine) in the district. This was where the sixth-grade graduates had to go if they wanted to continue in school. It was six kilometers (three miles) from the Grady Grossman School in Chrauk Tiek, so every child who wanted to go would need a bicycle to get there. Seven primary schools were supposed to feed students into the Bonteay Pranak Secondary School, but it only had ninety students enrolled, and most of them didn't finish seventh grade.

The school was closed when Kari arrived, so she went to find the principal. She finally found him sleeping in a hammock under his house. He told her his teachers used to live in the pagoda, but they had left when the government announced its intention to cut all teachers' salaries by 50 percent. "The government no longer cares about the quality of education," he said. "All they care about is saving money."

How did these government cuts affect the children at the primary school in Chrauk Tiek? Three first grades were crammed into two with seventy students per class, and two second grades were crammed into one class with ninety students. This eliminated a teacher, which saved the government money. She looked around at the school she had built in Grady's name and wondered aloud, "How would I feel if I sent my kids to school in the United States and I had to wait for someone from Cambodia to send money to pay the teacher?"

Kari felt a sense of clarity. Now she had the truth of it: the government simply didn't care. She was going to have to find a way for a government school to run effectively without the government.

Bonteay Pranak Secondary School was built by the Japanese government in 2004. In 2007 it was little more than empty building with standing water in the school yard and cows grazing the property. The teachers rarely showed up.

chapter nineteen

The Letters

Kari didn't want her school to be one of those donated schools that stood empty, but she never thought it would become her life. The project was slowly turning into a full-time job that needed much more support than she could generate by selling Cambodian silk scarves at Christmastime. And the peace and quiet of Lander suddenly felt like a pretty out-of-the-way place to headquarter an international development organization.

So, in the summer of 2007, driven by a passion to make the school she built work, Kari set a new course for her life with the support of her baffled husband. They uprooted their family and moved to Fort Collins, Colorado, to be closer to the Denver airport. Kari began traveling around the country to speak to people about what was happening in Cambodia. She told herself it wasn't that people didn't care; it's that they don't know. The children in Cambodia were invisible; the American media had no interest in Cambodia now that the U.S. military had no presence there.

As the fall leaves turned golden in Colorado, Kari sat in the office of a new home they'd rented in Fort Collins, talking to the Grady Grossman School's principal, Ngim

Sobun, half the world away. He had driven a moto two hours to Phnom Penh, and with Sovann interpreting, they were having their first free conversation using Skype. After seven years in Cambodia, Kari had learned one firm lesson: she didn't know anything about the problems of the people who live there or how to solve them, so she needed to listen to them. So she listened, and Sobun talked. From him, she learned that deforestation was a more pressing issue than school computers.

Principal Sobun tried to help her understand what was happening. "The natural resource in the Aural Mountain area, we are unable to protect because of the uneducated people who cut down all the trees to sell in exchange for rice and for money. Before, they just cut down the best timber for the houses and for the furniture, but this year they cut all kinds of trees, even the saplings, for charcoal and wood sticks for cooking every day. Each day they are destroying thousands of trees and hunting wild animals without any authority stopping them. They don't think about the future consequence for the children."

Kari knew that she needed to go back to Cambodia once again to witness this new roadblock in her attempts to keep her school open and operating properly. When she got back to Cambodia, the changes in the countryside were immediately apparent. The destruction was unbelievable. The forest canopy that used to cover the road was gone. Even the once familiar roads to the villages were different. They were rutted and filled with potholes, destroyed by heavy oxcarts carrying wood in the rainy season.

Sovann drove the van behind Principal Sobun, who negotiated the ruts on his moto through thick smoke and burning trees on both sides of the road. The fires were set on purpose to clear the land. They passed a deeply soiled mother and her three children washing dishes in a muddy, fetid puddle; the dry season remains of a creek bed was their only water source. Kari could only imagine what diseases they might catch.

The loss of the trees meant that when the rainy season turned to dry season, the river dried up faster. Not only was the forest losing its wild animals, but the people were losing their water. And that wasn't the only change. On the outskirts of the village, a thatch-hut settlement of newcomers had sprung up. Each family had a pile of hardwood stacked neatly by the side of the road in front of their hut, a harvest of cooking sticks for which the family earned $2.62.

When she asked Sovann to stop the van so she could talk to the people, one man told her that a government military commander paid him seven dollars per tree. That was five times a teacher's daily wage.

Because of all the newcomers who had moved into the logging camps, the Grady Grossman School now had 485 students in five classrooms. Sometimes there were over ninety students in a class and more leaning in the windows. Was there a student among them capable of becoming a lawyer to protect the villagers' natural resources? The logging was illegal, yet no one had the education to stop it.

When they got to Chrauk Tiek, the children and their parents gathered at the school for an assembly to greet Kari. Principal Sobun began the meeting with a village highlight: Chrauk Tiek students had won second place in the district soccer tournament, their very first sporting event! The claps and smiles conveyed their first taste of community pride. When it was her turn to speak, Kari asked the villagers what they wanted for their school. No one answered.

She wasn't sure if they had no opinion or if they didn't want to share it in a public arena. They just stared at each other in uncomfortable silence. The villagers seemed to be waiting for her to answer her own question, perhaps afraid to say the wrong thing. Since it was Kari's money, whatever she wanted was what they wanted. They'd most likely come to the meeting because they didn't want to miss whatever the *barang* (foreigner) had to offer this time. In their silence, Kari sensed the invisible reality of a donor's privilege and power.

She had brought books, educational games, and a new computer, but the villagers were more concerned about the illegal logging dividing their community. While the children played soccer barefoot in the schoolyard, community leaders told Kari the truth: Bun Vana, the forest community leader, had been evicted from his position the past July—in a secret meeting between four high-ranking officials—and replaced with a newcomer. The forest had been burning ever since. The trees were needed to retain water during the rainy season in order to support life during the drought season, but the villagers were powerless to stop the destruction.

"What if we ask everyone in the village to write a letter to protest this?" Kari asked.

They all shook their heads. No one knew how to write. No one can stop the powerful man.

"The ones who can write can sign their name," Kari said. "And the ones who cannot can thumbprint letters written by their children."

A few eyes opened wider with the possibility.

"You will put our lives in danger," Bun Vana said. A powerful, high-ranking, former Khmer Rouge military commander and close friend of the prime minister had moved his logging operation into the area. Bun Vana had expressed his frustrations about the problem with passion, but for all his efforts, the government had done nothing. His protests and those of the villagers he represented remained invisible.

At the next school assembly, Kari picked up a stick and said, "If one person writes a letter, you are easy to break." She snapped the stick in half. Then she picked up a whole bunch of sticks and said, "If everyone writes a letter, you cannot be broken." She tried to break the whole bundle of sticks, but it held strong.

The teachers and villagers were afraid to write a letter, but one visibly pregnant, soft-spoken woman said that she wanted garbage cans and water filters for the school. When the others had left, she handed Kari a neatly folded piece of paper, her letter expressed something completely different. She wrote of her deep concern about the lack of water, lack of income opportunity, lack of health care, and lack of law enforcement. And she signed her name—Thou Cham Sokah. The letter detailed the overthrow of community leader Bun Vana by a corrupt local authority, the newcomers who had come to cut down the trees, and the bribes taken from oxcart and wood truck drivers carrying whole tree trunks. Kari tucked her letter away, emboldened by the woman's courage.

Even the people who *wanted* to stop participating in the destruction had no choice. Transporting wood to the city was the only way many people could get enough money to feed their families every day.

Kari showed the men of the village Thou Sokah's letter and said, "If a pregnant woman can write a letter, then you can write a letter." They passed around the letter and mumbled in satisfaction, agreeing it was a good letter. They would try.

Equatorial rainforests are the lungs of the planet; we need the trees to provide oxygen to counteract the CO2 produced in industrial nations like China and the United States. Their wholesale destruction affects all people, as well as a diverse array of endangered species living in the Aural Wildlife Sanctuary that our planet may lose forever. Cambodians need to grow food, but without trees to hold the water and soil, they can't.

Kari never thought of herself as rich and powerful before she went to Cambodia, but compared to Cambodians, she was. Their government used its power to keep the people invisible and imprisoned in poverty. Kari's education was something she'd taken completely for granted, yet it had taught her how to be resourceful. She decided to use it to try to make Cambodians visible to the rest of the world. The future seemed doomed if she didn't.

The next day the children at the school busily worked on their letters. With colored pencils and glitter glue Kari had brought, they created vibrant drawings around neatly printed Khmer script, "Please Don't Destroy My Future, Don't Cut Down The Trees."

Proud children handed Kari their letters one by one and smiled. Many parents were afraid to sign their names because they live in fear of the corrupt police and military, but the children didn't care. Their letters featured hand-drawn pictures of the forest, animals, birds, fallen trees, muddy waters, and dead animals. Kari ended up with a pile of 178 letters from students and teachers; villagers added forty-eight more. Kari didn't know what to do with them, but she promised not to stop trying until someone noticed and agreed to take action.

Kari looked through papers in her hands—precious little seeds of democracy. She hoped that the voices of the children would touch the heart of the minister of environment and spur him to action. What an awesome responsibility to keep her promise and show the international community the environmental crisis and concern of the local villagers. She hoped she had enough evidence to interest some international reporters. Unfortunately, local Cambodian reporters took bribes to keep quiet about the forest. She knew the children's future depended on stopping the forest destruction and the corrupt governance tied to it. Everything depended on those letters.

Kari asked the teachers to educate the adults in the village about how they were being exploited, to teach students that paying bribes to break the law is wrong, to teach them how to decipher who is true and honest—to teach them to think. The Cambodian style of rote learning teaches students to copy, so the cycle repeats itself. They need to learn to think creatively. Kari brought a new computer, puzzles, Sudoku, and Rubik's Cubes to stretch their brains in new ways.

When Kari went home to Colorado a week later, she continued to work diligently to get the letters to as many news organizations as possible.

She was beginning to get depressed at the thought that her effort might be for nothing, when she received a call from Washington, D.C. The caller's name was Sok Khemera, a Cambodian reporter with the Voice of America. He planned to air her story in a week and dispatch a press release to Voice of America's media contacts around the world. On February 1, 2007, Kari turned on the Internet radio to hear Sok Khemera's report:

A surprising intervention tactic in Cambodia's ongoing battle against poachers and loggers has emerged among students in Kompong Speu's Aural District. The students say they're fed up with strangers coming and going—carrying axes and chainsaws, machetes and machine guns—illegally depleting the forests of animals and trees, apparently without fear. Students are drawing cartoons to highlight the effects of these crimes and are sending them to authorities in the hopes that something will be done in time...Nearly 100 primary school children, aged 10 to 16, drew cartoons, and many signed them. The bright, glittery drawings rebuke these illegal activities and explain why animals need the forest. They warn of animal extinction, flooding, and erosion. In their pictures, criminals saw trees while poachers kill wildlife. Mountains are bare, and the land is stripped clean...Kong Heang, governor of Kompong Speu, rejected the student's accusations. "There is no major illegal logging in Aural, he said, because much of the area is protected by strict measures from provincial authorities and the Ministry of the Environment, as well as non-governmental organizations. No big illegal logging occurs in this area..." But villagers say that armed forces like soldiers and the police, backed by businessmen, are those who actually cut down trees, confiscate land and, instead of protecting the forest, set up checkpoints to squeeze money from travelers. Meanwhile, a complaint signed by local men and women has been submitted to public and non-government agencies, giving the name, age, and address of signatories, some as young as five.

She listened to the broadcast and smiled. Her students were heard! The villagers had spoken out together with one voice, and no one was threatened or killed. It started with one brave, pregnant woman, Thou Sokah, who wrote the first letter. Something had changed, generating a spark of belief that the future could too. Little did Kari know that this brave act of solidarity was the first baby step toward empowering the community with the control to make their school reliable and accountable to *them*.

Thou Sokah hands Kari the first letter.

Students from Chrauk Tiek primary school gave Kari 175 letters about the forest destruction issue.

Old growth forest around Chrauk Tiek village around 2005.

Last tree standing 2007.

chapter twenty

Lessons Learned

In a living room in Breckenridge, Colorado, Kari was giving a talk about her dream to find a way to sustain a school in Cambodia economically, when a curious couple decided to take a chance on her belief that it could work. Bob and Elly Gordman were successful retail consultants who had taken an interest in her work after reading her first book, *Bones That Float*. They were intrigued by the social and entrepreneurial aspect of the idea of marrying small business with education. After the living-room talk, as Kari and George were selling books and Cambodian silk scarves to the crowd, Bob and Elly pulled Kari aside and said something that would change her life: "We want to donate five thousand dollars"—her jaw dropped—"for three years." She cried.

That's how Kari found herself on an airplane with her family on Christmas Eve 2007, traveling to Cambodia to spend their winter break learning how to make biomass briquettes for cooking fuel. "We're flying through the night with Santa," she told her children. Grady was in first grade, and he was excited to see the school that was his namesake. At three, Shanti was just excited to wheel her new princess backpack around the airport.

They were surprised to see some of the more cheesy aspects of Christmas being celebrated in Phnom Penh. A dinky, plastic Christmas tree with flashing lights adorned the entrance to their hotel, right next to the spirit house, a typical Buddhist decoration by the door. They were greeted with "Happy Christmas" by the hotel staff. Kari had felt a little guilty about making her kids spend Christmas in a hot, rural village in Cambodia, so she'd decided to splurge on a hotel with a pool in Phnom Penh for the week they needed to get over jet lag and help Sovann gather supplies for their trip to the school.

In Aural, cooking fuel has everything to do with education. One and a half million people in the capital city of Phnom Penh cook with wood sticks, and Aural is the largest and closest source of these cooking sticks. Chopping up hardwood trees for cooking fuel destroys the forest, funds a culture of corruption, depletes the water source, and keeps children out of school. Yet no one does anything about it.

The miserable looks of dirty-faced children sitting atop oxcarts full of logs spoke a sad truth. Kari desperately wanted the school to offer them another option. She had learned about biomass briquettes from the Legacy Foundation, an Oregon-based engineering development organization. Created from raw material collected from the ground—dead leaves, rice husks, sawdust, and waste paper—biomass briquettes are an efficient, low-cost cooking fuel. Sanu Kaji from the Foundation for Sustainable Technology in Nepal was coming to Cambodia to train the Chrauk Tiek villagers how to make them. Business can be a powerful change agent but aligning it with a mission to support rural schools was pioneering unknown territory. Kari's ambition to help villagers generate income to support their school sought to address the economic problem and the environmental destruction with a technical solution. However, there was also a social threat to this idea that she did not quite grasp.

For thirty years, survival depended on lying and suspicion. How can people work together for the common good when all anyone cares about is putting money in their own pockets? Traumatic memories of the Khmer Rouge regime and its aftermath embedded distrust in the social fabric.

When Kari arrived at the school, she was immediately petitioned to settle an argument. The teachers were mad at Principal Sobun for not paying a young woman with a 6th grade education to substitute for his first grade class. Nobody trusted him; they thought he kept the money sent for the teachers for himself. The teachers passively protested the principal's behavior by not showing up, taking long breaks, and drinking on the job. All this unrest over fifty bucks. Now Kari understood what "donor fatigue" meant; she was getting it too!

Donor fatigue was setting in because the problems felt endless. Kari had to remind herself to feel good about helping. She visited a classroom and shouted out Khmer letters with sixty first-graders. She taught second-graders how to use Play-Doh, LEGOs and K'Nex. She helped sixth-graders sound out words in English and taught them to sing, "If You're Happy and You Know It, Clap Your Hands." She paid a music teacher to give a blind boy private music lessons. She started Saturday English for the secondary students who didn't have access to language lessons. She showed everyone how to do jumping jacks. She enjoyed their smiles. She listened to them sing. And she prayed for the support she needed to keep it going until she could get the community to believe in the idea that the school was *theirs* to change.

Each day a villager showed up at school with some food to donate. Kari took it as a good sign that she was wanted. The first day she received a giant jackfruit, the next a black swan. The blind boy, Riat, brought her boiled taro roots, a snack time treat served with sugar. Kari bought a deer from a local hunter to supply them with meat for two days before it spoiled. The principal's wife, Sowin, cooked three meals a day with two clay pot cook stoves and a small wooden chopping block on the floor of a two room, thatch roof dwelling that she, her husband, and their 2-year-old daughter called home. No running water. No refrigerator. No electricity.

Kari and her family's intestinal tracts took it all fairly well. Grady, the native Cambodian in their family, got a bellyache due to accidental intake of water from the river they bathed in daily. His spiky fevers made Kari nervous about the threat of Dengue fever, an endemic disease that's spread by insects. Little Shanti didn't like the Cambodian nanny they had hired to keep her occupied. She was forlorn, but as long as she got to swim in the river every day and take a nap in the hammock, she reluctantly found contentment. Kari wasn't sure why she had brought her family to the jungle.

Each morning the students assembled in a half circle around the flagpole at 7 am to chant a Buddhist prayer and sing the national anthem, followed by a poor excuse for physical education class. A militant series of stiff postures with little movement: arms up, one foot forward, arms down, other foot forward, swing side to side, a lot of hands slapping against legs. It didn't raise Kari's heart rate one beat.

Sleeping on bare wooden planks made her stiff, so each morning while the children went through their militant exercise drill, Kari performed a series of yoga stretches on the cement portico of the school. After a few days of watching this, Principal Sobun asked her to teach the students yoga.

The strange yoga poses brought squeals of delight that lit up the schoolyard, reassuring her why she had brought her own children to Chrauk Tiek. They had fun doing it too. Kari recognized a girl with tight, curly hair who played the Ta Kay beautifully in music class and always sat in the front, eager to learn everything being taught. Helping her do warrior pose, Kari wondered if she would go on to secondary school next year. Most girls dropped out between sixth and seventh grade and only one or two might finish middle school. For real and lasting change to happen they needed kids born and raised there to become teachers. The problem was that no one ever stayed in school long enough.

Sanu Kaji trained 40 eager villagers how to make briquettes using pulped scrap paper, sawdust, and a simple wood and metal press. Kari thought the alternative cooking fuel meant they wouldn't have to cut down trees and they could sell briquettes in the market instead of wood sticks and raise money for the school. However, the results were not what she expected.

When the three-day briquette workshop concluded, the participants were more interested in their certificates of completion than the briquettes themselves. They had no interest in using briquettes for cooking because at home they could gather scrap wood. They wanted to make a product to sell in the city, not to use. Kari set Sovann up with a marketing budget to help the villagers find customers but it was too small to have any real impact on attracting buyers to their product. Even though they brought in a technology appropriate for the resources available, and the community had requested the training, Kari found she had made a classic mistake in assuming that a technological solution could resolve a social problem.

When the briquette business failed to generate income for the school, she got serious donor fatigue. She was disappointed in all the wasted time and money. She wanted to take her family home and never go back to Cambodia. The problem felt too big to solve but the hopeful smiles of the kids in her classrooms, and the haunting eyes of the kids riding atop oxcarts full of logs, kept her committed to figuring out what would work. She knew the learning opportunity was there, if she cared enough to find it.

Failure showed her where to begin. The community needed to believe in a common vision and work together, a daunting task when the lack of fifty dollars can tear a teaching staff apart. Everyone seemed to be in a perpetual argument over every little thing, with opinions cemented by debilitating jealousy. Kari was humbled to realize just how difficult it is to empower people. The village culture lacked solidarity, and the community lacked good leadership. Obviously, finding a way to sustain the school wasn't going to be as simple as one briquette project. The process didn't start with economic development or even environmental sustainability; it started with *human* development. Education and leadership were needed before sustainability would be possible.

Back home in the United States, people were reading her book, asking her to speak to them about the work in Cambodia, and handing her checks at the end of those speeches. The checks were getting bigger as Kari was getting more and more tired. She knew it would take a long time to nurture independence, and she knew that doing it alone was never going to work.

"If you're going to go on," George said, "you need to do it differently."

So Kari dropped the name Friends of the Grady Grossman School and renamed the organization Sustainable Schools International. She felt this name better reflected the intent of the organization: to make rural schools reliable and accountable to the local community whose children attend the school. She hoped the name would keep her focused and attract more support.

Kari also acknowledged that she needed help. The first thing she asked the newly formed board of directors to do was to find a way to give her a salary. She thought, "Cambodians are poorer than me, so I've put them first, but in the process I've made myself poor. George and I have burned through our profits from selling our house. I have no time for my children or for myself. I'm forty years old and I've gained twenty-five pounds in one year. My health is in the worst state of my life; I couldn't climb a mountain if I wanted to." This is not sustainable.

Kari and the board decided that a ten-year commitment was required. This would be long enough for local kids to become educated teachers and leaders capable of tackling sustainable solutions for their community. And if they were going to be in it for the long haul, Kari was going to have to be a part of the equation.

Almost as soon as they put the new name up on the website for Sustainable Schools International, schools in Cambodia, India, Brazil, Ethiopia, Nepal, and other nations started contacting them. Responding to the loud message that education is the path out of poverty, many concerned people all over the globe were building schools for the poor. The challenge now was to make sure those schools were in communities that could take ownership of them and find ways to support their children and teachers.

Biomass briquettes drying in the sun in front of the Chrauk Tiek Primary School 2008.

chapter twenty-one

Human Resources

Kari returned to Cambodia in October 2008 under the heady title of Sustainable Schools International executive director, a big name in an infant organization. She went to the city to interview a new English teacher, Rattana, a very impressive young woman. Since it's difficult to find an educated city person to work in a remote village, Kari wanted to find out if Rattana's interest was deeper than money, so she asked her why she wanted the job. Rattana said her family had moved from a rural village to Phnom Penh in hopes of finding work. Without education or money, they ended up living in the city dump; both parents and all seven children had scavenged the garbage to survive every day. When she was thirteen, Smile of a Child, a French group, rescued her and her siblings from the dump, and provided them with education and health care. She studied with them for eight years to gain a high school diploma and skills in sewing, computers, and English.

Rattana was a gracious and quick-witted young woman who might have been lost to the Phnom Penh city dump, surviving like a mangy dog until an even more exploitive situation swept her away. Families like Rattana's in the countryside often migrate to the city in search of work;

without literacy or job skills, they end up scavenging the dump to survive. Kari hoped she could teach the children of Chrauk Tiek how to avoid that trap.

The idea behind Sustainable Schools International is to stop this cycle where it starts, in the poverty of rural villages, where a well-functioning school is a lifeline to a different future. With Rattana as a role model, teaching fifty students elementary English six days per week, Kari hoped to instill a commitment to education in girls. English language skills have little use in a rural village, but a good English class increases the perceived value of a school, attracting the attention of parents and the attendance of students.

Kari met Rattana's parents on the day the two of them left for Chrauk Tiek. Her mother regarded Kari with graceful suspicion. Although Rattana was twenty-three years old, it was understood that her mother was the ultimate authority and made all the important decisions for her.

When Kari and Rattana arrived in Chrauk Tiek for the first day of school, Kari asked the parents gathered under a large acacia tree, "Who can read and write?" Two people raised their hands. She followed that question with, "What is the biggest reason children do not attend school?"

With Sovann and Rattana helping to write down answers, they collected thirty-eight surveys from parents. From the surveys, it was easy to conclude that the poor showing by teachers was consistent. Principal Sobun claimed he had no support from his community to deal with the problems. He had just fired three teachers, including the American Assistance English teacher, for watching pornography on the school's only solar-powered computer. There was zero expectation or reward for excellence in teaching from the provincial education department. And if officials got word that Kari was in town, someone showed up in a Land Cruiser and yelled at the teachers about doing a better job, never offering them resources to do it with. The teachers sat silent at those meetings, seething with resentment.

Principal Sobun, like most other principals, walked a line between doing enough for the school to function and thieving as much as he could. He was a government employee, so Kari had no choice but to work with him, but she believed he could do better. The parents' view of his behavior was critical to community involvement. If only he could see the value to himself of making the school serve the children first. He had three new government teachers for Khmer subjects, and Kari offered Rattana as the English replacement.

The community didn't have the authority to oversee the school or the money to enforce it, so Kari asked the parents to help create a performance-based incentive for the teachers. She offered thirty dollars to double each teacher's government salary if they showed up on time and sober. The students would take the teacher's attendance. If a teacher was absent, late, or drunk, one dollar was deducted. If teachers had more than five deductions, they lost the whole bonus. If they lost the whole bonus more than one time, they lost it for the rest of the year. Kari tried to insist that drunkenness was grounds for immediate firing and discovered that firing a drunken teacher was actually difficult. No one wanted to collect the necessary evidence because of how it would affect the fired teacher's family in this relationship-oriented culture.

To get Rattana acquainted with her new home, they walked together over the metal bridge to the market town where newcomers with money, mostly from the illegal timber trade, set up little shops and restaurants. They turned down the lane through the squalid loggers' camp. Families live there under miserable conditions, chopping wood and hauling water from the river seven days a week under a hot sun. There are no trees left to provide shade.

Beyond the logging camp is the old Souy village of Ca Peou, where mothers and grandmothers watch many dirty children running about while the men are off in the fields or forests from dawn until dusk. One mother beckoned Kari and Rattana toward her home, anxious to discuss a problem with her son.

Seventeen-year-old Sokea sat with his eyes downcast in the dirt while his mother explained how desperately he wanted to go to high school. When secondary school teachers didn't show up, he stayed and read whatever books he could find. He scored well enough on government tests to complete and pass grade nine. His parents had no idea how to make it possible for him to attend high school.

When Kari asked if he'd like to study in Phnom Penh, he looked up and smiled. She called an acquaintance who ran a boarding house for rural students in the city. His dormitories were surrounded by gardens growing fruits, vegetables, and medicines, and supplying all the produce needed to feed thirty-five students. A fishpond and chicken coop provided the protein, and on the weekends, his students worked his rice field to sustain themselves. If Sokea was willing to work one hour per day on his farm, he could live there. Kari agreed to provide a scholarship to pay the eighty-dollar "registration fee" to the Phnom Penh school and twenty dollars for a bicycle. His mother bowed and called Kari "sister."

Sovann protested, "Why you give scholarship to a boy whose parents are woodcutters?"

"If we don't want him to follow in his father's footsteps," Kari replied, "we have to give him the education to do something else." The forest was being felled by ignorance. Although Sokea's father was a member of the Human Rights Party, he didn't understand how natural resources and human rights were connected; he was only trying to survive.

"Give one student a scholarship, and you will make everyone else jealous," Sovann said, which annoyed Kari. She was aware of the Cambodian penchant for jealousy, but was she going to let it stop a bright kid from graduating from high school? What if he had the tenacity to become a lawyer?

The Chrauk Tiek community needed its children to become teachers, doctors, and lawyers—and Kari wanted the villagers to see real benefit from supporting them. She decided to have a "giving back" rule. The high school scholarship student's families had to volunteer at the primary and secondary schools, and the recipient themselves would work in the village for three to five years, depending on the amount of scholarship they received. If they served their time in the village after graduating, the loan would be forgiven. If they didn't, they would be expected to repay the loan.

"How we can force the scholarship recipients to come back and help?" Sovann asked.

Kari had no idea. She could only coach them on why it mattered and on the belief that they could change the miserable situation. The desire to do so had to come from within them.

Sovann had spent his life in a fierce competition for survival to escape rural poverty. Like Amanda, he had spent his boyhood living in fear and hunger as a slave laborer under the Khmer Rouge, but unlike Amanda, he never got to leave it behind. He fought and earned every inch he climbed up the economic ladder. Now he was a city dweller, and he wasn't going back to help his own village. How could Kari expect him to inspire a scholarship student to do it?

Sovann's hardscrabble life made him Kari's perfect requisition partner. He could bargain, negotiate, maneuver, and acquire anything from anyone. He was good at getting tasks done in a country where every little purchase, repair, and government interaction took so long it felt like they were working in molasses. He loved foreigners and used an extensive if not confused English vocabulary; his ability to communicate with Kari had made him a capable partner for many years. But rural villagers didn't respond to his demanding and authoritative communication style. Once Kari understood that they needed to develop a labor force with a better attitude, his street-smart strengths exposed his academic weakness. Sadly, he was also a victim of Cambodia's poor education system; he didn't have the skills needed to embody Sustainable Schools International's vision.

It wasn't Sovann's fault, but Kari's vision really couldn't be implemented by anyone who had lived under the abuses of the Khmer Rouge regime and never left the country. A three-pronged approach to education, leadership, and sustainability needed people with a generous and compassionate worldview. She had no idea what the potential of Sokea might be, but he inspired her to start leadership training. She hoped there would be more students like him.

Before Kari left for home to start figuring out how to raise money for more scholarships, a tiny, dark woman with wrinkled skin and red, betel-nut-stained teeth cornered her in the doorway of a classroom. Her name was Ya, and she had brought her son, Sarim. They were Souy minority people, the poorest of the poor. From beneath a worn and dirty krama headdress, her clouded eyes pleaded for her son's opportunity to go to high school. She told Kari how she had given birth to Sarim in the forest while on the run from the Khmer Rouge. He was her twelfth child, the fifth still alive, the only one to complete primary and secondary school. She was illiterate; her son wanted to be a math teacher. No Souy had ever gone to high school.

After arranging a place at the boarding house for Sokea, Kari picked up Sarim at the gate of his family's tiny hut on her way back to the city. Ya sent him off with the clothes on his back and a bag of rice over his shoulder. She handed Kari a sleeping mat she'd woven from palm leaves and held Kari's hands between hers, "I give my son to Angka (meaning Sustainable Schools International)." Kari got the feeling Sarim was now her son too.

Sarim leaves home with nothing more than a sack of rice on his back to become Kari's second scholarship student and the first Souy male to attend high school. His mother, Ya, saying goodbye.

chapter twenty-two

A Change of Attitude

Kari was furious when Rattana quit. Her mother had found her a second cousin in Long Beach to marry; she would be going to California to make donuts instead of being a teacher and a role model for rural girls. Brain drain. Rattana, a bright young woman who had lived in the dump and received an education from an aid organization would be leaving the country, taking her skills and her inspiring story with her to Long Beach. When organizations give education with no expectation of students giving back, many of them leave their home for the city or find a way to leave Cambodia altogether, rather than contributing their skills to help their home village grow. Cambodia desperately needs its educated people, especially the few it has from the underprivileged class.

In the newly painted library at the Chrauk Tiek school, Thou Sokah, the brave woman who wrote the first protest letter, was now serving as school librarian. She had only an eighth-grade education but that was enough to instruct a class of first-graders how to make their Khmer letters in the little wooden library outside. As usual, the classroom was overcrowded. After the students drew their letter on their slates, they raised them proudly to show the new librarian their Khmer script.

After the library lesson, the children checked out the new Khmer language books Kari brought and dove into the LEGOs and K'Nex. Thou Sokah introduced her to one of the boys, Da Vid, who had only one leg. She told Kari his family has no means of transportation, so his nine-year-old brother carried him on his back two kilometers (about one mile) to school every day.

She also told Kari how Da Vid had lost his leg: He was asleep in his family hut and got up to pee one night. The family had no bathroom, so he ambled in the dark to a nearby bush to do his business and startled a poisonous snake, which bit him. There was no doctor in the village to attend to the life-threatening bite, so Da Vid rode two hours on the back of a neighbor's moto to a hospital in Kampong Speu. His leg was amputated just above the knee to keep the venom from reaching his heart.

Da Vid showed Kari the white scar of his stump, with its fresh stitches. He said with a shy smile that it hurt most of the time. Because he was a growing child and his bone would continue to grow through the skin, he would need multiple amputations of the bone until he stopped growing. It would be all his family could do to keep up with the transportation costs to the free children's hospital in the city. The other children in his family might have to drop out of school to help.

"You are a brave boy," Kari told Da Vid. "What would you like to be when you grow up?"

"A doctor," he said. She gave the family a bicycle to make it easier for his brother to take him to school.

A Buddhist holiday closed the school for the next two days, so the parents gathered in a classroom for the first school-supporting committee meeting. In America, there are Parent Teacher Organizations (PTOs) and school boards; in Cambodia, they have school-supporting committees. But in Chrauk Tiek, the committee was only one person. Rather than reinvent the wheel, Kari decided to ask more people to join the school-supporting committee. Imagine a school board with no money or a PTO that raised money to cover teachers' salaries, and all the members are illiterate. Kari communicated with them using drawings on a chalkboard.

"What makes a good leader?" was her opening question. A heated discussion ensued about the meanings of *duty, respect, honesty,* and *transparency.* There was a lot of bickering and complaining about Hun Sen, the prime minister, and other corrupt leaders. Finally, Kari interrupted.

"Cambodia has a terrible government, and if you want that to change, you have to start here," she said, pointing to her head. "You can't change them; you can only change you. The kind of leadership that you show running this school is what these five hundred children will learn about leadership. If you show them good leadership, when they grow up they'll know the difference, and they may change the government. For now, we start here. We will all have gray hair by the time this is finished. But the children will have better jobs to care for you in your old age." That got their attention.

In the end, the parents found consensus in one goal: all students will achieve a high school education. With only two attending high school, this was going to be a long journey. Kari was worried how she would proceed with this goal. Then she met a Cambodian American who understood.

Paul Chuk had emigrated to the United States in 1979 from a refugee camp in Thailand after surviving the

Khmer Rouge genocide. Rebuilding his life in Florida meant mastering English at age thirty and finding work at a machine shop, where he worked his way up the ladder to supervisor. When his children graduated college, he felt called to return to Cambodia to see if he could help.

When he lost his job as a repairman in the recession of 2008, he decided it was time to go back to Cambodia and take his chances. He had saved enough money for an airline ticket and three months of living expenses. Almost sixty years old with no college degree, no one would hire him. He had found only a volunteer gig as an English teacher at a slum school that was run by a mutual friend. He called Kari out of the blue one night and met her outside her Phnom Penh hotel.

Paul appeared to be a typical city Cambodian, so she didn't expect him to be much help, but she still invited him to visit the school for a week and then decide if he could work there. To her surprise, he said he liked the place even though his accommodation was a small, dark room in the teachers' residence with two barred windows and a cement floor. Paul had no real teacher training, but within one month of teaching English at the Chrauk Tiek school, it became obvious that he was a gifted teacher–not just with students but with the whole community.

The first thing Paul addressed was the litter. Kari didn't see it; when she came to visit, Principal Sobun yelled at everyone to pick it up because the *barang* was coming. But what Paul saw every day was a sweltering mess of garbage and people who took no personal pride in their surroundings. And he set his mind to change it. He asked the students nicely and gave them good reasons to pick up: to make the school look and feel beautiful. He taught the teachers not to yell at the students but to stoop to the ground and work beside them. "Don't force them to do something you're not willing to do yourself," he said.

He showed Principal Sobun how to talk to the teachers nicely about helping with the garbage cleanup and to do his part instead of yelling at them from his position of power.

In a matter of weeks, no one had to remind the students to pick up the garbage anymore; they were proud of their clean school. Paul even attacked the fetid ditch full of trash rotting in standing water along the front gate, a breeding ground for malaria-bearing mosquitoes. No one could believe that a Khmer who had lived in America and spoke English would stoop so low and do such a disgusting job, and many students and some teachers jumped in to help. The neighbor who had created the stinking mess was embarrassed and agreed to help keep it clean.

As the schoolyard grew cleaner, hearts started to change. Soon the children were taking these ideas home and demanding that their families keep their area clean. They created garbage cans and recycling bins, and they scolded their parents if they didn't use them.

Village people respected Paul for how he behaved rather than for his position. Although he had no college degree, with his small frame, bald head, and Cheshire cat smile, he became known around town as "the professor." He was the best English teacher the school had ever had, and he cared passionately that his class started on time and the children learned something. The other teachers were watching his behavior, if not following it.

Paul didn't tell anyone what to do—he showed them. He sat in the school-supporting committee meetings but didn't say anything; he just listened and took notes. As he slowly worked himself into a trusted position, Paul never said a word about the problems he saw: alcoholism, violence, mistrust, closed-mindedness, selfishness, low self-esteem, abusive language, disrespect, fear, and controlling behavior. Instead, he asked a dynamic, young leadership trainer whom he'd met in Phnom Penh to come and teach a workshop about attitude.

Despite the fact that it was "stoong season," when everyone focused on the critical work of replanting rice seedlings into neat rows of paddies, twenty-nine people showed up for the attitude class. When the workshop began, the trainer asked the teachers, principals, and villagers to keep an open mind and to allow themselves to explore and absorb something new and interesting.

Drinking and violence had been the norm in Chrauk Tiek for generations, and often women were the victims. Their spouses abused them verbally and physically. Yet, they had no way to escape the abuse, no one to protect them; they were powerless.

"Is hitting a good way to show someone that you love them?" the trainer asked the class in a whisper. He paused for a few seconds of silence.

"No!" he screamed at the top of his lungs. People jumped to attention.

"To get better and find happiness, everyone needs to look closely into their own life and be willing to make some changes," the trainer told the group. For most villagers, it was the first time they had heard that something different was possible. In a culture full of dishonesty, resentment, unkind acts, hitting, greed, unhappiness, distrust, or conflict, they had to think about a better way to relate to each other. The participants left the class encouraged by the new meaning in their lives and imagining that happiness and prosperity would begin to sprout slowly around the community.

Rumors spread around the village of people drinking less alcohol, being more honest, and being less physically violent and verbally abusive. Paul's Cheshire cat smile bloomed when he heard the news. The foundation was set for progress to begin.

Paul Chuk joking with Chrauk Tiek students at the morning assembly.

chapter twenty-three

Dreams Grow Bigger

On Kari's next trip to Cambodia, in February 2009, she sat down with Paul during dinner. He devoured a plate of fried ants while they discussed how to change the principal's behavior to be more honest and transparent; how to make the teachers care about teaching; how to get the parents to participate and send kids to school; how to raise chickens, feed children, feed teachers. Together, Kari and Paul wondered how to find funds to expand the leadership program to other villages asking for help.

Under the principal's outdoor kitchen hut, a small group of villagers gathered to watch Kari eat and listen to her strange English words as Paul translated the gist of their conversation. At the edge of the darkness, where the warm glow from a single light bulb powered by a DC car battery didn't reach, sat the Souy leader Ek Chun, his wife, and their eight children. In a whisper to Paul, Chun begged forgiveness for not sending his children to school. He needed their labor to go to the forest and dig for wild potatoes; they'd been out of rice for two months. His children smiled in the dark night and stared at the pile of leftover rice in Kari's bowl. She couldn't offer it to them because it would shame their father in front of the others.

Instead Paul and Kari woke up the rice seller later that evening and purchased two fifty-kilo bags of rice. To avoid the attention of his neighbors, they coasted in front of Chun's home with the van lights off and, under cover of darkness, carried the two huge bags of rice down the long path to his thatch hut. Chun's wife clasped her hands around Kari's with a fierceness of a mother desperate to feed her children, pledging to use only two cans worth per day and make it last until their new rice crop could be harvested.

Chun showed Kari his empty rice barn and explained that he had to sell all the rice to pay for his ninety-five-year-old father's funeral expense. Funerals are so important in Cambodia that a family will starve to give an honored parent the chance of reincarnating into a better life. On the tiny porch of his thatch hut, around the glow of candlelight, they discussed their oldest daughter Saram. She was seventeen and missed the test to complete seventh grade while digging for wild potatoes. She would either have to repeat the grade or drop out. Kari knew the latter was likely.

"No matter what, this one must go to school," Kari said. Chun agreed not to marry her off.

Saram wanted to become a Khmer teacher and return to her village to teach. She was tired of the teachers not showing up. Before Kari took Saram to the boarding house in Phnom Penh, Saram couldn't even look at her or speak; she'd never been out of her village. She felt carsick the whole trip to the city because she'd never ridden in a vehicle either. She would join a growing number of scholarship students and eventually become the first Souy female ever to finish middle school, much less attend high school.

The city experience challenged the children they transplanted there in ways that forced them to grow confidence, to sink or swim in the urban world, to transform or go home. More than half of those who tried failed, but the ones who stayed possessed a determination that broke the mold of youthful Khmer shyness. The first time Kari saw the woodcutter's son, Sokea, outside his parents' cottage, kicking the dirt and wishing he could go to high school, he couldn't even look her in the eye. When she met him at his Phnom Penh high school he smiled, looked at her directly, and said in English, "Hello, how are you, madam?" It seemed like more than just a year had passed.

The high school was a very busy place, with more than four thousand students in six cement-block, three-story buildings. Sokea's class had sixty-six students squished into six rows of desks. They were studying geography, so Kari told the class she'd give a dollar to anyone who could tell her where Colorado is. The task would have been easier if they had a map or a globe, or at least a book, none of which were present. The teacher told her those teaching tools were downstairs in her locker.

The system works something like this: the teacher has the information, and if you don't pay the teacher, he or she doesn't give it to you. Sokea had to pay for his private "short course" in the afternoon to have access to the books, the globe, and the second half of the lesson. Kari met with the principal, who confirmed the system but told her if she would supply the names of the kids she supported, he would be sure they were exempt from the practice. "Pathetic," Kari thought. She didn't like the principal and wondered how much he was pilfering for his own personal gain.

In the absence of a map, Kari posed an easier question to the geography class: "Who is the president of the United States?" There were gasps and smiles and lots of hands raised. Kari picked a girl who perfectly and proudly pronounced "Barack Obama."

"What's special about Barack Obama?"

"He has black skin," she answered without hesitation.

When Kari gave her the dollar, she asked her to sign it. Black skin in Cambodia signifies hard labor in the hot sun, the common life of rural children, and is considered ugly and low class. To have a leader of the free world with black skin helped break a stigma. Now Kari wished she could just get a globe into the geography classroom. She wished that building a good education system in Cambodia was as simple as providing proper school supplies.

Paying short-course fees—or teacher bribes, to be more precise—would need to be included in scholarships from Sustainable Schools International. Kari didn't like the practice but couldn't fight it. City teachers weren't paid any more than rural ones; they just had access to students with money to pay them. City kids pay their teacher every day from first grade onward, just to get a seat in the class. They pay to take a test, they pay to get a grade, and they pay to pass. Teachers assigned to rural villages have families that are expecting a return on their investment, and the rural kids don't have the money to pay them. That's why teachers don't show up. Rural kids educated to be rural teachers is the only solution.

Their little workforce-development team had gotten bigger. With the addition of Saram, they now had six young people living at a boarding house in Phnom

Penh. All of them had been intimidated by urban people and ashamed of their dark skin and rural roots. Paul visited them often, counseled them on how to negotiate the urban world, and encouraged them to attend the attitude training workshops that his friend offered weekly. The students greeted Kari with big, bright smiles, and mustered up the courage to practice their English. "Before I have scholarship I was destitute, but after I take attitude class, I have hope," one of them said. A year before, they had no idea what they wanted to be. Now they're dreaming big.

Sokea, the first scholarship student, wants to study agriculture and rural development. Sarim, the Souy boy, wants to be a math teacher. Saram, the Souy girl, is attending eighth grade and hoping she can continue seven more years to become a Khmer teacher. Pally, an eleventh-grade girl, wants to be a medical doctor. Her brother, So Theara, wants to be an engineer. These were all human resources that the village needed, but Kari knew it would be a long while before they had enough education to return and enable real and lasting change in their village.

Paul had walked into Kari's life when she thought she couldn't go on, and so had Sem Kong, who brought the future closer when he requested assistance to go to college. Kong was twenty-five years old and had been out of high school for three years. His father was the village carpenter, who did his best to support his son's passion for schooling. Kong had walked more than five kilometers (three miles) every day to attend primary school, and after that he rode a rusty bicycle seventeen kilometers (more than ten miles) every day to go to secondary. All his brothers and sisters dropped out of school to help their mother with rice field work so that Kong could continue to high school. He was working manual labor in a cornfield from dawn until dusk for a few riels per day in hopes of saving enough to go to college.

"My life is so hard," he told Kari with his gaze fixed on her toes. "But I never give up my goal that someday I might have a chance to continue study." Kari had no idea when she gave him that chance that Sem Kong would go on to become Chrauk Tiek's first college graduate and Sustainable Schools International's first homegrown leader.

Kari commissioned a tuk tuk, a moto pulling a small carriage, to take the six scholarship students out on the town for a night. They stopped for dinner at her favorite claypot restaurant, where patrons chose from big piles of raw meat and vegetables, and cooked it themselves in the soup pot in the middle of the table. The kids gorged themselves on what they called "big food."

For entertainment, Kari took them to the Sorya shopping center, a newly built vertical mall that rose above Phnom Penh like an alien apartment complex. Riding escalators up five stories was an adventure; Saram was scared to step on the moving steps, so she gripped Kari's arm. At the top, they stepped outside the restaurant to the observation deck overlooking the city. The students stared wide-eyed at the vast cityscape and gaped at the tiny cars and people below. Seeing the breadth of the world for the first time, their dreams grew bigger. Kari hoped they would embrace the vision she was trying to share and carry it forward. The pace of their progress would be determined by when the students felt ready to lead.

chapter twenty-four

Five Core Values

Two village chiefs, sixteen members of the school supporting committee, and over three hundred villagers sat under the shade of two old army parachutes for a "thank you for building the fence" ceremony. Principal Sobun ran through a list of accomplishments, and Paul used his loudspeaker to call up each volunteer. Kari let them choose a thank-you gift from a pile of sweatshirts and pants she had collected from the lost and found at her children's school back home in Colorado. Clothing that was never even missed by her kids might be the only outfit these children would wear day and night until it turned into unrecognizable rags.

Paul and Kari shared the stage with representatives of three nearby villages who were hoping they would expand their program to their schools. An official from the provincial Ministry of Education told them, "The most important thing is community participation and the honesty of the school principal."

Kari looked at Principal Sobun, whom she knew was neither honest nor transparent, and hoped he'd find the incentive to straighten up. The ministry official was impressed with the high level of community participation and said he would contact the World Food Program about starting a school breakfast. Kari wondered why the basic need to have a teacher present in the classroom every day wasn't his top priority.

She tried to express what she had seen in the scholarship students' eyes to the parents in Chrauk Tiek, but apparently she didn't need to; the same energy was enlivening the village primary school. Children were coming to school early and staying late because it was the most happening place in town. Their happy screams permeated the air from dawn until dusk, generating talk in the community about exciting possibilities.

Then an amazing thing happened. One by one, villagers took the microphone and pledged their support, whether it was helping with the school breakfast, contributing an oxcart of wood sticks for the cooking fires, cleaning up the school grounds, or contributing food to the teachers, for the first time they talked about doing something to make a better future for themselves.

Sem Kong's father, the village carpenter, asked, "What can we do for the ones who already drop out of school?"

Different people had different ideas: sewing, mechanics, beautician, a power tiller for agriculture, a pond for every house. They were not only thinking, they were also speaking out. "Now we're getting somewhere," Kari thought. After that meeting, more people showed up for the school-supporting committee meetings, though few of them could read. The strategy to overcome the deep divides in the community was a set of five core values: participation, communication, honesty, trust, and solidarity.

Kari drew a symbol for each word on a large piece of paper and laid it on the ground. She gave each person ten beans to place on the symbols to grade their feelings about each of the five core values. Then they counted the beans. There were no beans on honesty or trust.

"What can we do to increase trust?" she asked.

"Participation," one person shouted out. "Communication!" insisted another. Everyone started pointing to the pictures, moving beans and drawing arrows. A picture emerged. Participation was the starting point; an arrow led to communication and then to honesty, to build trust in order to create solidarity. Kari was stunned by the self-generated feedback of a handful of illiterate adults, a more useful analysis of a problem than all the PhDs at the United Nations could come up with. She clapped. They clapped.

"Will you spread this information to the other villagers?"

"Ja!" (yes), shouted the women.

"Baat!" (yes), shouted the men.

She realized she finally had willing role models. The labor force was growing.

"We were in the dark," one man said as he left for home. "Kari brought us the lantern."

What she didn't know was that these five core values— participation, communication, honesty, trust, and solidarity—would be put to the test with every single thing they tried. Paul's daily presence as a Cambodian with an alternative attitude was crucial to helping the community learn what the values meant. The school breakfast was the first test.

The World Food Program (WFP) requires a community that's active, honest, and organized. This is a tall order for traumatized rural villagers in survival mode. Only two schools in the district qualified. World Food

Program inspectors could show up at any time and shut down the program if any food was missing.

Three women had to show up at four every morning to cook the school breakfast, standing over hot fires to stir vast cauldrons of rice and fish soup in the pre-sunrise darkness for a salary of fifteen kilos of rice per month. They didn't have a bicycle to get from their hut to the school or even a light to see their way and cook breakfast by. The villagers were supposed to build themselves a storage barn, kitchen area, and large-scale cookstoves, and provide the cooking utensils, with nothing but a few small pots provided by WFP. Paul worked with the community to gather and purchase the equipment for the volunteer cooks and wondered why the WFP didn't understand the basic needs of their program. The principal and two volunteers got three days of training on how to requisition the food and cook it. Then they were on their own.

Problems surfaced immediately. Sokah, the librarian, held the key to the stock room. She portioned out the exact ration of food for the cooks to prepare each morning. Each day she opened exactly nine cans of mackerel and tomato sauce, specially formulated to fight malnutrition. She had four kids at the school and wasn't going to allow anyone to mess it up. She marked the open rice bags to make sure nothing was stolen, which put her in conflict with Principal Sobun.

The principal was constantly hassled to pay rice kickbacks to the distribution network above him. The "power man" in this case was a government employee called Duon. It was Duon's job to make food requests to the WFP and deliver it to the schools. He demanded rice payments from recipient schools for his own use. Sobun tried to cut three malnourished kids from the take-home food rations, stealing from the most powerless to fulfill the power man's demand, but Paul wouldn't let him do it. Duon made the principal's life difficult by invalidating paperwork, refusing to answer questions, and threatening to find something wrong that would shut down the program, Principal Sobun was distraught.

"This is the way the system works," he told Paul. "You can't change it."

Kari went to Phnom Penh and met with the WFP country director. Within twenty-four hours, field monitors showed up to investigate. Paul told them everything. It wasn't the first report of Duon's rice-stealing shenanigans that they had heard. When the field monitors left, the angry and worried principal told Paul, "This change is too fast; they could kill you."

Kari didn't want to put Paul's life in danger either. "I don't care if they kill me," Paul said. "I am an old man. I have lived through the Pol Pot years. What more can they do? If we don't stand up for the children, who will?"

The principal was in a very difficult position; they required him to be honest, and his government bosses required him to be dishonest. When government employees are corrupt, villagers resist passively by refusing to participate. Resistance can be confused with laziness. Without participation, people don't communicate, and then village solidarity spirals downward. Corruption undermines a community's ability to be honest and build trust.

The breakfast had increased attendance to capacity, even during the harvest season. The teachers said the students concentrated better and were smarter. At 6:30 a.m., the kids started showing up at school with their plates and spoons in hand, then played on the playground and cleaned the schoolyard until a metal rod hit the rusty tire rim that serves as a school bell. No one was late.

At 7:00 a.m., each teacher was stationed around the schoolyard with a five-gallon bucket of mackerel bean soup and rice. The WFP contributed the fish, beans, and rice, but the children didn't like the taste, so every week a different class took its turn bringing in a papaya to add to the soup. Each child walked to the well to wash his or her dish—even the five-year-olds—an activity supervised by a handful of sixth-graders who made up the student council. No janitor or lunch ladies were there to pick up after them.

A few months later, the World Food Program managed to fire Duon, who no doubt had family connections tied to his position. Paul was pleasantly surprised. "It's you they're afraid of," he told Kari. "You're American, and here that represents so much power that everyone is afraid of you." That made her very proud to be an American.

Community members vote on the five core values by placing beans on the pictures that represent the words.

chapter twenty-five

"Wash Hands Soap"

Roamvong is a Cambodian dance. A large group up of people gyrate slowly in a circle around a center point while twirling their hands from the wrist. Khmers look graceful doing this, and Westerners look like clowns. Rented karaoke speakers blasted Khmer love songs at a deafening volume into a dark schoolyard at the first school dance, held in honor of the first-ever Sanitation Day. The kids ruled the *roamvong* circle as parents watched from the periphery. Outside the circle of light, the littlest children had already fallen asleep on the ground in the darkness, exhausted from picking up after the adults who fouled their school yard with plastic wrappers, fruit peels, and cigarette butts.

Two drunken policemen were dancing. They were the worst people in town but had to be invited to provide "protection" anyway. Paul and Kari were afraid one of the drunks might fall over and discharge the AK-47 strapped on his back. Three doors down from the school gate, the civilian police and military police sat drinking and gambling all day, while day and night, oxcarts stopped in front of their small thatch house to pay bribes for the illegal logs they carried from the forest. They had fat bellies, and a disgusting squalor of garbage surrounding their outpost. They complained the loudest when Paul turned off the music at 10:00 p.m.

The next morning was Sanitation Day. Three hundred students fanned out into the village to pick up the garbage that filled every yard and alley in Spean Dyke, the little market town across the bridge. They started the sanitation work at the hung-over military policeman's house.

Thankfully, Kari had brought eight pairs of leather work gloves as gifts for the men on the school-supporting committee. She donned a pair and pitched in, picking up copious amounts of plastic, straws, shoes, rice bags, old clothes—a long list of nasty debris. The job was completely disgusting but with a swarm of people working yard by yard, alley by alley, it was done in three hours. Even the village chief joined in picking up other people's garbage, and Kari was proud of him. It was a strong statement in a culture with a rigid socioeconomic hierarchy.

Pile after pile of garbage was burning in all directions, and it stunk. Paul walked up and down the road with a bull horn, politely instructing business owners to help maintain a clean town. He explained how important it is for the children to be healthy so they can go to school. A little embarrassment went a long way. Some of the stingy market people offered them water, and the policemen promised to help enforce trash pickup.

Through the acrid smoke of garbage fires, the cleaning crew walked back to school down the middle of the dusty road, singing, "If you're happy and you know it clap your hands." When the song ended, everyone broke into a chant, "*lian dy saboo*" ("wash hands soap"), and went to the well to do just that.

That evening, after sharing a few snacks at her favorite ramshackle, roadside dessert stand, Paul and

Kari walked through Spean Dyke under a blanket of a thousand silent stars, keeping pace with a creaking caravan of oxcarts hauling whole tree trunks from the forest. Their police neighbor approached the side of the road with his flashlight, intending to collect bribes. Paul and Kari pretended he was there to greet them, taking great pains to compliment him for supporting the children and their efforts to keep the town clean. They distracted him until all the oxcarts had passed without stopping to pay him. He spot-checked them with his flashlight but was culturally obligated to continue to receive their compliments. They told him what a wonderful example he had been to the whole community by keeping the garbage under control, and then they walked away, satisfied that on this night, they had stood between him and his quarry.

The school committee members gathered to prepare dinner in the cooking shelter next to the stock room. They fixed a mountain of fresh vegetables, hand-pounded sweet brown rice, and a freshly caught chicken, skinny but delicious. It was a whole new experience in "free range." Ek Chun, the small Souy leader, started to sing a beautiful, tone-bending Khmer love song. One by one, each villager sang, expressing Khmer culture's unique, pleading innocence. The best Kari could offer was a few John Denver songs and "Oh My Darlin' Clementine." The song exchange felt both tribal and spiritual, like a celebration of the connection between them, regardless of their differences.

Both the villagers and Kari were a little mystified by what was happening. The kids were changing, expressing a level of joy and confidence they had never been seen before. More and more children wouldn't allow their parents to keep them away from school. One girl cried for half a day when her parents took her to a wedding celebration and broke their promise to have her back to school on time for class. A first-grade girl who broke her leg on Sanitation Day cried from the cot where she lay recuperating, not in pain but because she would miss a week of school.

The children used to be nervous, avoiding eye contact and shying away from Kari. Now they looked her in the eye, talked to her, touched her, and even asked questions. There was a lightness of being about them that can only be described as the cumulative effect of happy moments mixed with a growing sense of personal power. Education made them believe they could do anything.

The fifth- and sixth-graders showed up early the next morning, a day off from school, and started to work in small, organized groups around the schoolyard. They arrived with whatever tools they could scavenge from home: a hacksaw, an axe, two small planers, a few pencils, and small chunks of hardwood. Their mission was to turn the bits of dense, red tumloap wood they found on the ground into 150 little wooden crosses. A donor had offered to buy them at two dollars apiece for Easter gifts.

The school supporting committee had told Kari they couldn't do such a thing without training. "It's two sticks that intersect each other," Kari had told Paul. "Let's see if they can figure it out." She had given the children no resources at all, only the problem and the incentive of winning five dollars for the best design.

The three winning students were in charge of teaching the others how to produce the crosses, overseeing teams of four students, each whittling away with whatever tool they had until the wood resembled a cross. Next, the sanding teams worked to make the crosses smooth by rubbing them vigorously against the cement floor of the school. When the work was complete, Kari paid them three hundred for the 150 crosses, and Paul gave them the choice of taking home two dollars for each cross they made or keeping the money together.

To their surprise, the students chose to keep the money pooled and held a serious discussion and democratic vote to decide how to spend their money. Hauling water by hand every day with a bucket hanging off a bamboo stick that cut into their shoulders was hard work that took time out of the school day. A water cart big enough to carry fifty gallons would reduce this daily chore, so that's what they bought. With a few thousand riels left over, they bought a little paint for the water cart and wrote on the side of it: "Donated by the 5th and 6th grade class 2010." Kari felt certain it was the first time such a thing had happened anywhere in Cambodia. The decision-making experience became an important part of the process toward empowering the students to improve their school on their own.

When Principal Sobun returned from a district meeting and reported that the Provincial Education Department had chosen Chrauk Tiek Elementary School as the number-one school in the district, his face beamed with a proud smile. He hosted a meeting for representatives from other schools to exchange ideas and to foster improvement. Visiting teachers observed many things that their schools didn't have: a principal and teachers working together; a teacher residence; a schoolyard free of garbage; a modern bathroom; a kitchen and stockroom; breakfast for the children; a water tank; a playground; an incinerator; shade huts and trees; a vegetable garden; flowers; every student with his or her own book for each subject; and decorated classrooms. They wanted to know how to get these things.

400 students from Chrauk Tiek Primary School fan out into the fetid market town of Spean Dyke to clean up the garbage.

chapter twenty-six

Expansion

Kari used to believe that schools in Cambodia needed a computer, solar panels, and a generator, plus a satellite dish to connect to the Internet, because that's what you need to set up email pen pals with sister schools. That's what was important to her. Turns out, that's not what was important to them. A fence is important to them. And sustainability means working with what's important to them. Who knew that schools in Cambodia don't need computers nearly as much as they need power tillers?

Aside from teacher absenteeism, the main reason kids dropped out of school was that the demands of farming and daily living must be done by hand. Access to a simple piece of modern farm equipment to do the work instead of the children meant that jobs around the school got done faster, less work for kids meant more time for school, and renting out the power tiller generated a little income.

The villagers seemed to have an endless stream of uses for a power tiller. During planting season, it plowed the fields; during growing season, it pumped water for irrigation. While broken computers and abandoned solar panels collected dust in other schools, a two-thousand-dollar investment in a power tiller empowered the Chrauk Tiek School to plant one hundred dragon fruit trees for consumption and sale once they bore fruit. It cleared bushes and prepared the ground to grow sweet potatoes, cabbages, and the favored vegetable "morning glory" to help feed teachers. It hauled poles from the forest to build fences and gave the poorest families machinery to get farm work done. Earnings from the power tiller rentals covered the cost of gas, the operator, and equipment repairs, leaving fifty dollars in earned profit. The return on the investment of respect was a significant change of attitude.

When the new school year began, all the neighboring schools remained closed for several weeks because the teachers hadn't shown up, while the Chrauk Tiek teachers had returned two weeks early to get their school ready. Principal Sobun loaded the eighty-six-year-old music teacher, his students, and their traditional musical instruments onto the power tiller, and paraded the school band through the village streets with a crowd of students marching behind to encourage everyone in the village to bring their kids to school on opening day.

No one had to be cajoled into helping anymore; the teachers willingly pitched in and worked as a team, spending days clearing weeds from the schoolyard by hand for lack of a lawnmower. Villagers helped trim overgrown tree branches along the entrance, and several families brought wood poles to complete the dragon fruit project.

Principal Sobun listened closely to his teachers for new improvement ideas, rather than ordering them around. Two teachers brought younger siblings from their home villages to live with them so they could attend a good school. For teachers, it became more than a school; it was a family.

Principal Sobun had to turn away many children from neighboring villages who wanted to enroll, because the school had run out of room. The disappointed parents asked for another building to house more students, but that seemed like a waste of money to Kari. The neighboring villages already had foreign-donated school buildings, but they were empty most of the time. One of them held the only middle school option for her sixth-grade graduates wishing to continue to seventh grade.

Despite the unwelcome pressure of raising more money to meet the need, Kari decided to expand her education, leadership, and sustainability mission to two more villages: the primary school in Sre Chrap two kilometers (one mile) east, to relieve the overcrowding problem, and the secondary school in Bonteay Pranak, six kilometers (three miles) west. Bonteay Pranak had another primary school attached to it, which made for a total of four schools. She didn't want to build false hope, and she fretted over her commitment to open access to a continuum of education for 1,500 children and make it sustainable. She knew that the first thing she had to do was breathe life into their yellow buildings.

Kari was very encouraged by how far she'd come in Chrauk Tiek and was also reminded how far she would have to go when she started working with the secondary school down the road in Bonteay Pranak. The school was bare, and no children played in the dusty, treeless yard. No wonder her graduates were begging to repeat sixth grade.

She met with a group of villagers about the idea of strengthening their school-supporting committee. More than half of the sixteen people who showed up were illiterate women. Like moms everywhere, they wanted their kids to have a good school. Kari listened to the women closely and drew pictures of their vision on a flip chart. She was surprised that they dreamed of having a high school. The attendance in secondary school was so low that less than 10 percent finish ninth grade. The typical age of middle school students is sixteen to nineteen, and at that age, they're needed to work.

First Kari explained the five core values: participation, communication, honesty, trust, and solidarity. Then she passed out beans to find out the women's opinions. Honesty and trust held no beans—no surprise. The discussion shifted from priorities like cement fences, playgrounds, and buildings to happy, well-supported teachers.

"What does it take to support a teacher?" Kari asked. One-time expenses like housing and a bathroom were easy to tackle, but ongoing expenses like food, water, and salary would require a commitment and a change of attitude. Few people believed there would be no corruption. The secondary school principal had been pilfering from the school for years.

Principal Sobun bravely stood up to speak, admitting openly the mistakes he had made in the past and how it undermined community trust. In front of everyone, he told the secondary school principal he couldn't expect people to help him if he had bad behavior. People who had been conditioned for years to distrust everyone, assume corruption always, and look for handouts from humanitarians, started to discuss how to reach their goals together.

A demonstration of their commitment would start with a fence—a practical, achievable goal proved necessary by the cow that entered the school room during the meeting. Who'd want to go to a school with cow droppings in the classrooms? Fence building was a huge undertaking that required more community participation than this village had ever organized. The villagers had to overcome a grudge they held toward the principal for all the wood posts they'd already donated that had disappeared.

The villagers collected hundreds of wooden posts from the forest, and the students dug two-foot post holes in the hard ground by hand all the way around a schoolyard the size of two football fields. The sixth-graders from Chrauk Tiek led by example, digging holes in the extremely hard ground under a hot sun with great determination. With Paul modeling good leadership, the fence was built in five days.

The secondary school principal looked at the fence he had been trying to get built for five years and said, "It is an exciting day. From today we can progress."

Students building a fence to keep the cows out of their school yard and classrooms.

chapter twenty-seven

Seeds of Change

Sustainability is about helping people in the way they want to be helped. Unfortunately, one of the biggest factors stacked against the poor can be the very people trying to help them. Well-intentioned humanitarian aid from developed countries often has unintended side effects.

Thoughtless giving makes villagers believe there's no reason to help their school, because "the Angka" (outside organizations) is rich and will do everything for them. To avoid this, Kari asked the villagers two questions: "What is the problem you see at the school?" and "How would you like to solve it?" As they began to embrace their community power and speak their truth, they found themselves fighting the international humanitarian aid system that holds their corrupt government in place.

Once Kari started helping the neighboring primary school in Sre Chrap, the U.N. World Food Program asked that their principal give rice rations to twenty of the poorest kids. But he had no idea how to choose the lucky few, because every family in the village was poor and hungry. He knew it would create jealousy, divide the fragile solidarity of the school-supporting committee, and undermine their desire to work on projects at the school. He asked Paul to help.

Paul listened to the Sre Chrap villagers' concerns and wrote down what they wanted to express to the WFP. They spoke their truth and bravely asked the United Nations to give them something they actually wanted. That took courage.

They said,
1. The poorest families are poor because they are lazy and playing cards all day.
2. They do not value education.
3. They will get the rice and stop study.
4. They will get the rice and exchange it for money to buy palm wine.
5. If these people get the benefit, it will make the other poor people who participate in supporting the school jealous.
6. It will break down solidarity in the community support of the school.
7. It will make more trouble and problems to solve.
8. Our opinion is to offer school breakfast for the whole school first.

The community didn't want to give rice rations to twenty families, because they saw it causing conflict in their community. They wanted a breakfast at school to benefit all the children equally and increase their attendance. They were committed to doing all the hard work to pull it off.

On the Sre Chrap villagers' behalf, Kari went back to the WFP office in Phnom Penh and spoke to the country director, a Canadian named J. P., and his Cambodian colleague, Bun Thang. She told them that the Sre Chrap community didn't want food rations for a few; they wanted a school breakfast for all. J. P. seemed genuinely interested in this grassroots information and told her they wouldn't force the program on the community. But Bun Thang, his Cambodian counterpart, told her that the community's concerns were unfounded, because the program was based on World Food Program criteria: 80 percent school attendance was required to receive a take-home ration. That made Kari laugh. In a school where the teachers didn't even attend 80 percent of the time? As if he didn't know attendance records were made up for the sake of their "criteria."

Apparently, the idea of a community saying no to the WFP was novel, and no one knew how to handle it. Officials from the provincial education office showed up with their WFP counterparts to speak to the Sre Chrap villagers. It was a surprise visit, and the principal didn't have time to find Paul to help him. The Sre Chrap villagers were *afraid* of the government officials; they wouldn't speak their truth to people from the city who drove up in lily-white Land Cruisers, wearing dress pants and shiny shoes. Kari had told Bun Thang not to talk to the community without Paul, because he lives there, he has a relationship with them, and they trust him. But this advice was forgotten or simply ignored.

Being scared silent, the Sre Chrap villagers said nothing, but the officials made it clear what they wanted and effectively forced the community to concede to their take-home ration program. For ten years, no official had cared if the Sre Chrap school had a teacher. Even now they didn't seem to care if their teacher had housing, food, or a salary. What was their newfound motivation for feeding the poorest of the poor in Sre Chrap?

Kari suspected that someone was profiting. World Food Program food distribution is the responsibility of education department officials. The more tons of rice under their supervision, the more they could steal. So there was a U.N.-funded program acting like playground bullies. Why couldn't a U.N. program simply ask the villagers what their "criteria" would be?

Consider the incredibly difficult position the Sre Chrap principal was in. The WFP policy was based on school attendance. That means they would rely on the school principal to enforce the policy—the very same man who needed the community to help him build a fence and support the teachers, because the government didn't. If the community got upset, they would stop volunteering altogether. He really needed their help.

"If we control the attendance criteria, then will you accept it?" the WFP official asked, although he didn't say how he would enforce it and he didn't offer to live in Sre Chrap, which would be the only effective way to enforce it. He didn't call for a vote. He didn't ask if anyone was against it. From their silence, he concluded everyone was for it. The officials drove off in their Land Cruiser.

A few days later, the principal called a meeting to ask the Sre Chrap villagers to help him select the twenty families to receive a take-home ration. Only one person showed up. The community voted with their feet. The principal was practically in tears. Neither the education department nor the WFP seemed to realize what a critical role the principal plays in the relationship between the school and the community—and how rare to have one who actually cares.

How can a food distribution program for the poor be based on student attendance when you're working with a government that doesn't properly provide for teacher attendance and their food needs? Kari was beginning to get a sense of the enormous, invisible wall that these poor, marginalized villagers were up against. Because U.N. aid is required to be distributed through the Cambodian government, it is not only ineffective, it's counterproductive. It's the glue that keeps the status of power imbalance in place.

If we are going to help people in the way they want to be helped, we need to let the villagers speak and respect their answers. It's their children. It's their school. Show them that you trust them and that you are trustworthy. These are the seeds of change.

Student eating breakfast provided by the World Food Program.

chapter twenty-eight

The Return

A crowd of children lined the entrance to the Chrauk Tiek School, cheering and high-fiving Kari's return to Cambodia in 2011, ten years since her first visit. They held signs they made in English for her benefit: "Welcome back Kari," "You are Beautiful," "We Miss You," "Thank you for coming back again." A school brimming to capacity with happy children and smiling teachers—that's all the thanks she needs.

At the end of a long line of excited children, Paul emerged to welcome her with his Cheshire cat smile. "You are the queen of Chrauk Tiek," he said with a big hug.

"And you are its prince," she replied.

While no one in Chrauk Tiek understood why a Cambodian refugee who made it to America would ever come back to live in their wretched town, Paul told Kari he was the happiest he'd ever been in his life. "You empower me," he said. And in turn, he empowered everyone around him. He found healing for his own traumatic past in the legacy he was instilling in the children of Chrauk Tiek. He was a role model of integrity and tough compassion, behavior so rare Kari wished she could clone him.

However, reliance on Paul for guidance and Kari for money was not a sustainable way for Chrauk Tiek villagers to educate their children. Paul and Kari both knew that. Now that the first school was functional and Kari had expanded the program to three more, she needed to figure out how to work herself out of a job. In short, she needed more Pauls. What she got was even better when Sem Kong, the son of the village carpenter, became Chrauk Tiek's first college graduate. Paul took him under his wing as if he were his own son.

Paul, Kong and Kari sat in hammocks under the thatch roof of a riverside restaurant discussing the next steps for their new schools. A snack seller greeted them quietly, offering a large plate of honeycomb filled with baby bees and dripping with honey. Paul and Kong claimed it was juicy and delicious. "Bee larvae will make your heart strong," Kong said as he wiped a drip of honey from his chin.

"I don't eat bugs," Kari replied, "adults or their offspring." Implementing their vision of sustainable education was going to take all the strength of heart they could muster, with or without bee larvae.

Kong's family were poor farmers, his sisters and brothers having dropped out of school to help his parents generate income. The whole family sacrificed so one could get an education, and Kong took the responsibility very seriously. He was a trailblazer in his family: the first to graduate, the first to ride an airplane, the first to visit America.

"America is heaven for all the people of the world, but everything is very expensive," Kong said, recalling his visit to the promised land. "If my country became like America, maybe it will be perfect."

After Kong's graduation from a two-year course in English and computers at Phnom Penh's Western University, Paul brought Kong to Colorado to train for his job with Sustainable Schools International (SSI). After landing in Fort Collins, during its annual summer festival, a three-day block party called New West Fest, Kong's first job for SSI was selling iced tea. He couldn't believe anyone would pay $2.99 for a glass of tea, much less donate their change—from one cent to twenty dollars—to fill up a donation jar. The line of thirsty customers was never-ending. Perfect strangers donated money for his village in Cambodia—how could he explain such a thing? It was the biggest gathering he'd ever seen, yet people were polite, kind, honest, friendly, and modest. He was introduced as SSI's first college graduate, congratulated, and welcomed. It was unbelievable.

"This is really good," Kong thought, admiring all the bicycle lanes on the Fort Collins streets. "All the people respect the bikers and walkers, not like my country." In Cambodia, the minority rich drive luxury SUVs, and since bikes and feet are transportation for the majority poor, the rich would just as soon run them over as share the road. It was the first time he experienced a society where all people understood their duty to respect the law equally.

Kong attended an SSI board meeting and watched the directors argue fiercely but respectfully about how to spend the money raised. Even though he couldn't follow all the English, he was impressed by their honesty and intensity of purpose. How was a boy from a remote, rural village to give his opinion on how operations in Cambodia would manifest a vision of sustainable education? He trusted the passionate board would find the best solution.

"Without you, my life can't have this day," he thought. "Maybe I would be just a poor farmer and can't make a good future like now. I'm training to become a leader. When I return to my country, I have to use this experience to build up my school so my community can become strong. I'll show them the reason why SSI has been trying hard to help us."

New questions danced in his head. To find good solutions, we need the villagers' input, but where do we start? How can we convince them to bring their children to school and care about education and their children's future? How can the community stand up to eliminate corruption and bribes? What if the villagers lost their land or didn't trust each other? How do we observe the real situation to know what they need and how we can help them? All the problems could be solved with community wisdom, if we work with them to find the right way. Kong had never been taught to think or behave this way before, and he felt inspired by possibility.

His return to Chrauk Tiek had a strong impact on his own life and his village. When the villagers heard that Kong, a poor farmer's son, had graduated college and gone to America, SSI's message attracted great attention. He felt compelled to help his community understand and use the five core values: participation, communication, honesty, trust, and solidarity.

The Bonteay Pranak Middle School was a desolate building desperately in need of attention if it was to keep the kids from Chrauk Tiek in school before they lost hope and dropped out. Paul introduced Kong to students, teachers, and principals in Bonteay Pranak, and they were keenly interested in what he had to say.

He felt emboldened, and as he began to tell his story, his voice got very loud.

"I never gave up going to my classes, although I had much trouble in my family," Kong said. "I never gave up my belief that someday I might have a chance to continue my education. I was born to a poor family just like you. You shouldn't believe what people tell you— your family is poor farmer, so you shouldn't try hard to study, because in the future you must be like your family. That is not true. I heard this since I was young from all my community, but I didn't believe them. Your future is in your hands. If you give up and don't fight to study hard, then maybe you will become the same as your family like your community tells you. Now, with SSI supporting your school, you have a chance to continue your education and come back to help your community grow up."

And he added, "If I can do it, why can't you do it?"

The teachers and students clapped to congratulate him. As he started to work with Paul to pick up the garbage around the schoolyard, he hoped they believed what he had said. Watching men they respected pick up garbage inspired the students to help until the yard was spotless. Then they cleaned the bathrooms and classrooms, and decorated their classes. The next day Paul and Kong led the middle school students in digging up dirt and building a foundation for a teacher house. As they worked together for many hours in the hot sun, Kong was happy to see the cooperation he had inspired. Even the teachers joined in to help them.

He wanted to share with the teachers everything he had learned from his visit to an elementary school in Fort Collins. The Cambodian schools lacked so much in comparison to American schools, which had everything: printing paper stacked up to the ceiling, school supplies, a huge lunch room, computers, and all the school equipment available to teachers and students. He remembered how plentiful their environment was, and his heart ached for the poor students around him. He thought, "If they were given the same opportunity to go to a school with passionate teachers, good curriculum, and all the volunteers to help out, they too could do well in school."

They had almost nothing to work with, but he was determined to inspire everyone—parents, principals, teachers, and students—to do more to improve their schools. He was accepted throughout the community because of his sincerity, honesty, and commitment to change things for the better. He played an important role in building trust among villagers from different levels. Small but important changes were happening, motivated by a new belief in the people around him.

A successful and respected businessman in Bonteay Pranak helped purchase all the wood and supplies needed to build a teacher house. He traveled around the village, telling his friends and neighbors they should try to get involved in supporting SSI. "We need a good school for our children," he told them, "SSI can't do it alone. Kari, Paul, and Kong can't do alone. I want to give my kids a chance to earn a good education so they will do better than me." He hoped for a computer class so his kids could help him learn how to use a computer to run his business, but he understood they needed to work together to make a good school for all. More families offered to help, and several gave wooden poles from their stockpile to build a kitchen for the teachers so they can cook and store food and kitchen supplies.

Parents started to encourage their children to stay in school instead of helping them chop down trees, believing for the first time that a new job beyond working hard labor was possible. Secondary students who lived far away were no longer embarrassed to stay at school during their midday break, they brought rice and dried fish in a plastic bag for their lunch. This used to indicate they were poor, but now they were considered smart to save time and work on their homework.

"I am lucky to be at this secondary school, because SSI is behind it," the new geography teacher said. "I'm willing to do whatever is necessary to help build this school." She came from a very poor family herself and felt determined to share her life stories and to pass on her knowledge to her new students. At least they wouldn't be forced to drop out for lack of a teacher anymore.

All the teachers had changes of attitude. A third-grade teacher from Chrauk Tiek Primary told the teachers in Bonteay Pranak Secondary that they should work hard not for Uncle Paul or Kong or Kari, but because "we are doing this for ourselves."

"I'm very impressed with SSI's vision and principle," the new English teacher said.

Students were motivated; they spent more time reading books in the library. The teachers were happy and excited` to see the progress, especially their new house. They hoped their new attitude would attract villagers to participate in school activities and help raise money to buy small things the school needed.

As the villagers gathered for their school-supporting committee meeting, Kong counted ninety-four people, an SSI record. They came not because the *barang* was there, but rather because one of their own was there to lead. The main topic was community involvement. Kong talked about his experience in America, and he talked about how they needed to change. He told them the story of his work on the teacher house at Bonteay Pranak

Middle School, how he hired a bulldozer to bring in fill dirt for the foundation. The operator told him it would take two hours, but he would charge SSI for three hours on the receipt and they could split the overcharge profit.

Kong said he had smiled and firmly said, "No."

"The Angka has a lot of money," the bulldozer operator complained. "It's okay to make some money for yourself."

"No, it isn't," Kong replied. "That is going to change. When we cheat someone trying to help us, we cheat ourselves. You should be happy that SSI is willing to help your school, and you should also help your school and give one hour for free."

The villagers applauded his honesty and his intensity of purpose. They could trust him.

Sem Kong, age 25, SSI's first college graduate and homegrown employee.

chapter twenty-nine

The Secret to Sustainability

Paying government teachers a living wage remained an enormous challenge. Teachers made only thirty to fifty dollars per month from the government and it wasn't enough to live on. At two schools, Kari paid a salary bonus, based on teacher attendance, of one hundred dollars per month, but a real living wage would cost three hundred per month per teacher, and they didn't have enough funds to pay that, especially at Bonteay Pranak where there were twenty teachers. No one in the village made that much money, so it was unrealistic to expect them to spend much time earning it for the teachers. The power tiller business, the dragon fruits, and the guest huts for SSI visitors were all generating income, but it wasn't consistent enough to pay teachers monthly. The uneducated villagers found their solution in banking.

Microloans of fifty to five hundred dollars were increasingly available through various organizations and banks, focused on the popular practice of lending to the poor. But Kari was shocked to find out that microborrowers were paying 3 percent monthly, or 36 percent per year—and they consider it a good deal! Banks in this business make a killing, and altruistic institutions such as Kiva pay back individual donors for loaning their money. Paul observed that this was the only viable way to generate enough income to pay teachers monthly. Using his own money as startup capital, he invented the Community Prosper Bank.

To allow the Chrauk Tiek villagers to create their own banking policy, Paul and Kong formed a fifteen-member lending group that offered the same loan sizes and rates as other lenders in the region with the intent of using the interest to pay teachers' salaries monthly. Teachers were members of the lending group as well and were charged with the responsibility of doing the bookkeeping. The system allowed small-business owners to get their own credit needs met and generate income to pay teachers at the same time.

Since the members controlled the bank openly and transparently, enforcing its policies through the social pressure that judges a person's reputation in the community, it became popular quickly. Kong had learned to use QuickBooks and Excel spreadsheets while in America, so he recorded the policies and created repayment schedules for all the borrowers. The members could see who repaid and how much money was generated, then vote on the payment to teachers. Access to loans helped support an ever-growing number of skilled workers produced by the schools.

One woman who had dropped out of school after fourth grade but often taught first-graders the alphabet when government teachers didn't show up, completed a new sewing class offered at Chrauk Tiek school and opened her own sewing shop across the street from the secondary school at Bonteay Pranak. She got a loan from the Community Prosper Bank to buy a nonelectric sewing machine, which she operated by moving a treadle with her feet. Business was so good she could hardly keep up with her orders. She got another loan for fabrics and felt empowered that her loan payments would help pay the teachers.

Her success sent a strong signal to new students in the sewing class, girls who had already dropped out of school. They were eager to complete the course and open their own shop. They begged Principal Sobun's wife, the sewing instructor, to teach them seven days a week and skip holidays.

Kong was a good role model, and the villagers and their children were starting to think and work in new ways. Now the students in this remote place believed they could improve their community.

That's the secret to sustainability.

Paul and Kari talked about the number of scholarship students they had coming up the ranks and how they would train them to be leaders like Kong. They felt confident and relieved that there was a light at the end of the tunnel.

Once these human resources are ready and the schools they came from are sustainable and reliable to the local community, they plan to take that light and change education in rural Cambodia forever. No more empty schools. No more absent teachers.

They are still on that journey.

Kari being greeted by the children at Chrauk Tiek School, March 2012.

Epilogue

Empty schools are a worldwide problem. Many schools are built in poor countries without any resources to run them. The lack of teachers is a major reason why cycles of rural poverty persist. Seven schools in the remote Aural district of Cambodia alone are waiting for our help. Often we think that if we throw more technology or money at a problem, a solution will emerge. It won't. There is no silver bullet to speed up the development of the human heart; it can happen only at a human pace. That's why we need many more people to get involved. We need to have the humility to see the problem through the eyes of the poor, share our knowledge, share our fairness, and care enough to stay committed for the long haul.

You can help Sustainable Schools International help them by getting involved with MAKE CHANGE MATTER, a service learning program where you learn how the choices you make can have lasting impact on a child in Cambodia…and beyond.

Go to MakeChangeMatter.org and take action!

make CHANGE matter

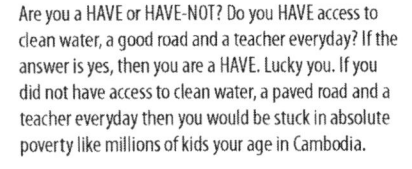

Are you a HAVE or HAVE-NOT? Do you HAVE access to clean water, a good road and a teacher everyday? If the answer is yes, then you are a HAVE. Lucky you. If you did not have access to clean water, a paved road and a teacher everyday then you would be stuck in absolute poverty like millions of kids your age in Cambodia.

What if...

...you showed up to school and there were no teachers?

...you had to pay the teachers yourself in order for them to show up?

...the only bike your family owns is old and rusty, and it takes an hour and a half to get to school?

...you had no way to get to school because the road to school is flooded with a foot of water?

...there is no water at your school, making it impossible to clean the bathroom?

...your parents need you to help them grow food by digging in a field with no tools other than your hands instead of going to school?

...you never have breakfast before going to school?

Meet the HAVE-NOTS. Many kids in Cambodia do not have access to clean water, a good road or a teacher everyday. The only way they will get out of absolute poverty is if some HAVES are willing to help them. Are you? Do you live in a country where education is free, teachers show up everyday, and they care that you learn? A global citizen learns how to bridge the gap between us and them by learning to understand the needs of children whose circumstance is very different than your own.

You Can Help...

You can help us make education possible for kids in Cambodia through our M&M program. All you have to do is fill up M&M containers with quarters — one container holds 56 quarters — enough to provide books for a school. If you get your friends or class involved you could donate much more — maybe even enough to pay a teacher's salary for one year. Here are the steps to starting the program:

1. Get the Containers.

For the M&M youth fundraising program, you can buy Mini M&M containers at most supermarkets. You can either hand out the tubes to your classmates or sell them for $1.00 to recoup your cost of purchasing them, your choice. When you give or sell someone a tube, put a label on it (click Teacher Toolkit at MakeChangeMatter.com to download labels). Make an agreement with them that they will return the container to you filled with quarters. Check periodicaly to make sure you get it back! The fun part comes next... eat those M&Ms!

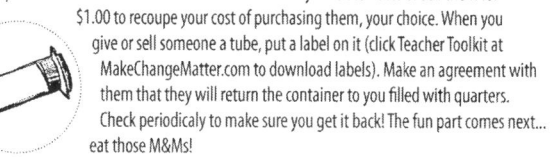

2. Collect Quarters.

Now that you've emptied out your tube, you can start filling it up with quarters. Here are some ideas for collecting quarters:

- Ask friends and neighbors to donate.
- Do chores. (Download our Chores Chart at MakeChangeMatter.org for suggestions on chores and to track your earnings).
- Organize a walk-a-thon, bike-a-thon, or any kind of -a-thon! Ask friends, family and neighbors to pledge a quarter for every lap, mile, or number of cars washed.
- Sell Something! Set up a lemonade stand, sell home-made cookies, list some old toys on ebay, organize your own or group yard sale — then donate the proceeds.

3. Send in Your Donation!

Once you've filled up your M&M tubes, we ask that you convert the quarters to a check or money order, made out to Sustainable Schools International. Sending a check or money order protects the contribution you have generously given. You can mail checks or money orders to: Sustainable Schools International, 236 Walnut Street, Fort Collins, CO 80524. Please include your contact information and email address so we can thank you!

Sign up for our e-newsletter on the Make Change Matter website so you can see the impact your donation has on the children in Cambodia.

Learn more about the M&M Program at MakeChangeMatter.org

Kari Grady Grossman is the Founder of Sustainable Schools International and the author of *Bones That Float, A Story of Adopting Cambodia*, which won the 2008 "Peacemaker of the Year" Award from the Independent Publishers Association, and was named a Gold Memoir by the Nautilus Awards for "World Changing Books."

Prior to writing her book, she spent nearly a decade traveling, writing, and producing documentaries that appeared on Animal Planet and the Discovery Channel Online, including coverage from Mount Everest and the Alaskan Iditarod.

The author is a 1990 graduate of Syracuse University and lives in Fort Collins, Colorado with her husband George and their two adopted children, Grady from Cambodia, and Shanti from India. In 2008, the Colorado Parents' Day Council named her and her husband "Colorado Parents of the Year."

Teacher Absent Often was adapted for young readers by Jennifer O'Neal Michel from Kari Grady Grossman's original work *Bones That Float, A Story of Adopting Cambodia*. Kari will expand part three of *Teacher Absent Often* to create her next adult work, *Sustainable Schools: A New Model for Success*.

Jennifer O'Neal Michel is an avid reader who enjoys nothing more than curling up with a good book. She works from her home in the Utah mountains, where she also enjoys spending time with her husband, Marlon, her two kids, Kacie and Dillon, and the family dog, Lizzie. When she has a break between books, she also enjoys her daily workouts, experimenting with new recipes, and making quilts. This is her first book adaptation.

READ THE AWARD-WINNING BOOK THAT INSPIRED *TEACHER ABSENT OFTEN*

Bones That Float
A Story of Adopting Cambodia
BY KARI GRADY GROSSMAN

Bones That Float—a Cambodian phrase for the sacred that rises above the suffering—is a heartbreaking tale of hope.

Independent Publisher's Book Awards,
2008 Outstanding Book,
PEACEMAKER OF THE YEAR

2008 Nautilus Book Awards
"Changing the World
One Book at a Time"
GOLD AWARD – Memoir
SILVER AWARD – Multicultural

Available at:
BonesThatFloat.com
Amazon.com

ISBN: 978-0-9792493-0-3

"This rare book, despite its harrowing truths, is an effective and hopeful call to action – a nudge to your social conscience that will have you asking, 'What's my Cambodia?'"

Angel Limb, *Artsline Editor* WCVE-FM 88.9 Public Radio, Richmond, Virginia

"Told with fierce honesty and an affecting voice..."

Loung Ung, author of *First They Killed My Father* and *Lucky Child*

"Impossible to put down and haunting long past its end..."

Violeta Garcia-Mendoza, *Rainbow Kids E-Magazine*

"A literary gem that employs sumptuous prose..."

Cathryn Alpert, author of the novel *Rocket City*

"The universal story of every human on this earth..."

Arn Chorn-Pond, musician, human rights activist, and star of the award winning PBS documentary film *The Flute Player*

Made in the USA
Charleston, SC
12 July 2012